OSHA Construction
Safety Checklist

Raúl Ross Pineda

OSHA Construction Safety Checklist
© Raúl Ross Pineda
Chicago, Illinois, USA
V.1 April 2021
ISBN: 9798738539206

Contents

Introduction 1
Safety Inspection 3
Subpart C—General Safety and Health Provisions 5
    §1926.21—Safety training and education 5
    §1926.25—Housekeeping 5
    §1926.28—Personal protective equipment 5
    §1926.34—Means of egress 5
    §1926.35—Employee emergency action plans 5
Subpart D—Occupational Health and Environmental Controls 7
    §1926.50—Medical services and first aid 7
    §1926.51—Sanitation 7
    §1926.52—Occupational noise exposure 8
    §1926.54—Nonionizing radiation 8
    §1926.55—Gases, vapors, fumes, dusts, and mists 8
    §1926.56—Illumination 9
    §1926.57—Ventilation 9
    §1926.59—Hazard communication 9
    §1926.62—Lead 10
    §1926.65—Hazardous waste operations and emergency response 12
Subpart E—Personal Protective and Life Saving Equipment 13
    §1926.95—Criteria for personal protective equipment 13
    §1926.96—Occupational foot protection 13
    §1926.100—Head protection 13
    §1926.101—Hearing protection 13
    §1926.102—Eye and face protection 13
    §1926.103—Respiratory protection 14
    §1926.106—Working over or near water 14
Subpart F—Fire Protection and Prevention 15
    §1926.150—Fire protection 15
    §1926.151—Fire prevention 15
    §1926.152—Flammable liquids 16
    §1926.153—Liquefied petroleum gas (LP-Gas) 17
    §1926.154—Temporary heating devices 17
Subpart G—Signs, Signals, and Barricades 19
    §1926.200—Accident prevention signs and tags 19
    §1926.201—Signaling 19
Subpart H—Materials Handling, Storage, Use, and Disposal 20
    §1926.250—General requirements for storage 20
    §1926.251—Rigging equipment for material handling 20
    §1926.252—Disposal of waste materials 21
Subpart I—Tools—Hand and Power 22
    §1926.300—General requirements 22
    §1926.301—Hand tools 22
    §1926.302—Power-operated hand tools 22
    §1926.303—Abrasive wheels and tools 23

§1926.304—Woodworking tools..24
§1926.305—Jacks-lever and ratchet, screw, and hydraulic..24
§1926.306—Air receivers..24
Subpart J-Welding and Cutting..25
§1926.350—Gas welding and cutting..25
§1926.351—Arc welding and cutting..25
§1926.352—Fire prevention...27
§1926.353—Ventilation and protection in welding, cutting, and heating...................27
Subpart K-Electrical...28
§1926.403—General requirements..28
§1926.404—Wiring design and protection...28
§1926.405—Wiring methods, components, and equipment for general use..............29
§1926.407—Hazardous (classified) locations..30
§1926.416—General requirements..30
§1926.417—Lockout and tagging of circuits..30
Subpart L-Scaffolds..31
§1926.451—General requirements..31
§1926.452—Additional requirements applicable to specific types of scaffolds.........36
§1926.453—Aerial lifts..37
§1926.454—Training requirements...38
Subpart M-Fall Protection...39
§1926.501—Duty to have fall protection..39
§1926.502—Fall protection systems criteria and practices...40
§1926.503—Training requirements...42
Subpart N-Helicopters, Hoists, Elevators, and Conveyors...43
§1926.552—Material hoists, personnel hoists, and elevators......................................43
§1926.554—Overhead hoists..43
§1926.555—Conveyors..43
Subpart O-Motor Vehicles, Mechanized Equipment, and Marine Operations................44
§1926.600—Equipment...44
§1926.601—Motor vehicles..44
§1926.602—Material handling equipment...45
§1926.603—Pile driving equipment..46
§1926.604—Site clearing...47
§1926.605—Marine operations and equipment...47
Subpart P-Excavations...48
§1926.651—Specific excavation requirements...48
§1926.652—Requirements for protective systems..49
Subpart Q-Concrete and Masonry Construction...50
§1926.701—General requirements..50
§1926.702—Requirements for equipment and tools...50
§1926.703—Requirements for cast-in-place concrete...51
§1926.704—Requirements for precast concrete...51
§1926.705—Requirements for lift-slab construction operations..................................52
§1926.706—Requirements for masonry construction...52
Subpart R-Steel Erection..53
§1926.752—Site layout, site-specific erection plan and construction sequence........53
§1926.753—Hoisting and rigging..53
§1926.754—Structural steel assembly...54

§1926.755—Column anchorage..54
§1926.756—Beams and columns..54
§1926.757—Open web steel joists..55
§1926.758—Systems-engineered metal buildings..55
§1926.759—Falling object protection..55
§1926.760—Fall protection...55
§1926.761—Training...56

Subpart S-Underground Construction, Caissons, Cofferdams and Compressed Air........57
§1926.800—Underground construction...57
§1926.801—Caissons...57
§1926.802—Cofferdams..57
§1926.803—Compressed air...57

Subpart T-Demolition..58
§1926.850—Preparatory operations..58
§1926.851—Stairs, passageways, and ladders..58
§1926.852—Chutes..59
§1926.856—Removal of walls, floors, and material with equipment...................59
§1926.858—Removal of steel construction...59
§1926.859—Mechanical demolition...59

Subpart U-Blasting and the Use of Explosives...60
§1926.900—General provisions..60
§1926.902—Surface transportation of explosives..60
§1926.904—Storage of explosives and blasting agents...60
§1926.905—Loading of explosives or blasting agents...60
§1926.907—Use of safety fuse..60
§1926.909—Firing the blast..60

Subpart V-Electric Power Transmission and Distribution..61
§1926.951—Medical services and first aid..61
§1926.963—Testing and test facilities...61
§1926.964—Overhead lines and live-line barehand work.....................................61
§1926.965—Underground electrical installations..61

Subpart W-Rollover Protective Structures; Overhead Protection...............................62
§1926.1000—Scope..62

Subpart X-Stairways and Ladders..63
§1926.1051—General requirements..63
§1926.1052—Stairways...63
§1926.1053—Ladders..63
§1926.1060—Training requirements..64

Subpart Y-Diving..65
§1926.1076—Qualifications of dive team..65
§1926.1080—Safe practices manual..65
§1926.1081—Pre-dive procedures..66
§1926.1082—Procedures during dive..67
§1926.1083—Post-dive procedures..68
§1926.1084—SCUBA diving..69
§1926.1085—Surface-supplied air diving..70
§1926.1086—Mixed-gas diving...71
§1926.1087—Liveboating..71
§1926.1090—Equipment...72

§1926.1091—Recordkeeping requirements..75
Subpart Z-Toxic and Hazardous Substances...76
   §1926.1101—Asbestos...76
   §1926.1127—Cadmium..77
   §1926.1153—Respirable crystalline silica...79
Subpart AA-Confined Spaces in Construction...81
   §1926.1203—General requirements..81
   §1926.1204—Permit-required confined space program..82
   §1926.1206—Entry permit..83
   §1926.1207—Training..83
Subpart CC-Cranes and Derricks in Construction..84
   §1926.1402—Ground conditions...84
   §1926.1403—Assembly/Disassembly— selection of manufacturer or employer procedures.
....84
   §1926.1404—Assembly/Disassembly— general requirements (applies to all assembly and disassembly operations)...84
   §1926.1407—Power line safety (up to 350 kV)—assembly and disassembly.........................84
   §1926.1408—Power line safety (up to 350 kV)--equipment operations................................85
   §1926.1412—Inspections..85
   §1926.1415—Safety devises..85
   §1926.1416—Operational aids...85
   §1926.1417—Operation...86
   §1926.1419—Signals—general requirements..86
   §1926.1422—Signals—hand signal chart...86
   §1926.1423—Fall protection...86
   §1926.1424—Work area control..86
   §1926.1425—Keeping clear of the load..87
   §1926.1427—Operator training, certification, and evaluation...87
   §1926.1428—Signal person qualifications...87
   §1926.1431—Hoisting personnel...87
   §1926.1432—Multiple-crane/derrick lifts—supplemental requirements............................88
   §1926.1433—Design, construction and testing..88
   §1926.1435—Tower cranes...88
   §1926.1441—Equipment with a rated hoisting/lifting capacity of 2,000 pounds or less.....88
OSHA Most Frequently Cited Serious Violations Construction Industry FY 2020...................90

Introduction

This checklist was developed as an aid for assessing a construction worksite's compliance with OSHA's *29 CFR, Part 1926, Safety and Health Regulations for Construction*.

This list is organized in groups of questions that follow the same nomenclature and order of the subparts of Part 1926. These questions are formulated in full sentences, closely mimicking the original text of the regulations, and each one includes its precise citation in the same regulations.

This checklist touches on fundamental requirements and is not inclusive of all safety and health requirements for employers in the construction industry. However, in most situations it will not be necessary to use a safety inspection checklist as comprehensive as this one. This document is intended to be taken as a starting point to be tailored to fit the needs of specific inspections; more often by ignoring unnecessary subparts and questions.

It closes with *OSHA Most Frequently Cited Serious Violations Construction Industry FY 2020*.

Safety Inspection

Company Name: _____

Jobsite Name: _____

Jobsite Location: _____

Date/Time: _____

Current Weather Conditions: _____

Superintendent/Supervisor: _____

Inspector: _____

The following questions may be answered by marking on its left one of those three options:

✔	An affirmative answer;
✘	A negative answer, or
N	The question is not applicable.

Subpart C—General Safety and Health Provisions

§1926.21—Safety training and education.

Is each employee instructed in the recognition and avoidance of unsafe conditions and the regulations applicable to his work environment to control or eliminate any hazards or other exposure to illness or injury? 1926.21(b)(2)

Are employees who are required to handle or use poisons, caustics, and other harmful substances instructed in their safe handling and use, and made aware of the potential hazards, personal hygiene, and personal protective measures required? 1926.21(b)(3)

§1926.25—Housekeeping.

Is form and scrap lumber with protruding nails and all other debris kept cleared from work areas, passageways, and stairs? 1926.25(a)

Are combustible scrap and debris removed at regular intervals during the course of construction? Are safe means provided to facilitate such removal? 1926.25(b)

Are containers provided for the collection and separation of waste, trash, oily and used rags, and other refuse? 1926.25(c)

Is garbage and other waste disposed of at frequent and regular intervals? 1926.25(c)

§1926.28—Personal protective equipment.

Are employees required to wear appropriate personal protective equipment when there is an exposure to hazardous conditions? 1926.28(a)

§1926.34—Means of egress.

Are exits so arranged and maintained as to provide free and unobstructed egress from all parts of the building or structure at all times when it is occupied? 1926.34(a)

Are exits marked by a readily visible sign? 1926.34(b)

§1926.35—Employee emergency action plans.

Are the following elements, at a minimum, included in the employee emergency action plan? Emergency escape procedures and emergency escape route assignments; procedures to be followed by employees who remain to operate critical plant operations before they evacuate; procedures to account for all employees after emergency evacuation has been completed; rescue and medical duties for those employees who are to perform them; the preferred means of reporting fires and other emergencies; and names or regular job titles of persons or departments who can be contacted for further information or explanation of duties under the plan? 1926.35(b)

Does the employer establish an employee alarm system? 1926.35(c)

Does the employer establish in the EAP the types of evacuation to be used in emergency circumstances? 1926.35(d)

Before implementing the EAP, does the employer designate and train a sufficient number of persons to assist in the safe and orderly emergency evacuation of employees? 1926.35(e)(1)

Does the employer review the plan with each employee covered by the plan initially when the plan is developed? 1926.35(e)(2)(i)

Does the employer review the plan with each employee covered by the plan whenever the employee's responsibilities the plan change? 1926.35(e)(2)(ii)

Does the employer review the plan with each employee covered by the plan whenever the plan is changed? 1926.35(e)(2)(iii)

Is the written plan kept at the workplace and made available for employee review, or for employers with 10 or fewer employees is the plan communicated orally to employees? 1926.35(e)(3)

Subpart D-Occupational Health and Environmental Controls

§1926.50—Medical services and first aid.

Does the employer insure the availability of medical personnel for advice and consultation on matters of occupational health? 1926.50(a)

Are provisions made prior to commencement of the project for prompt medical attention in case of serious injury? 1926.50(b)

Where life threatening injuries could occur, is a facility for the treatment of injured employees reasonably accessible in terms of time and distance to the worksite? If not, is there an employee(s) trained in first aid at the site? 1926.50(c)

Are first aid supplies accessible? 1926.50(d)(1)

Are telephone numbers of physicians, hospitals, or ambulances conspicuously posted in areas where 911 emergency dispatch services are not available? 1926.50(f)(1)

Are suitable facilities provided where needed for quick drenching or flushing of the eyes and body within the work area for immediate emergency use where the eyes or body of any person may be exposed to injurious corrosive materials? 1926.50(g)

§1926.51—Sanitation.

Is an adequate supply of potable water provided at the worksite? 1926.51(a)(1)

Is a common drinking cup prohibited? 1926.51(a)(4)

Are outlets for nonpotable water, such as water for industrial or firefighting purposes only, identified by signs meeting the requirements of subpart G of this part, to indicate clearly that the water is unsafe and is not to be used for drinking, washing, or cooking purposes? 1926.51(b)(1)

Are toilets provided for employees in adequate number? 1926.51(c)(1)

Does the employer provide adequate washing facilities for employees engaged in the application of paints, coating, herbicides, or insecticides, or in other operations where contaminants may be harmful to the employees? Are such facilities in near proximity to the worksite and equipped to enable employees to remove such substances? 1926.51(f)(1)

Are washing facilities clean and sanitary? 1926.51(f)(2)

Are employees prohibited from consuming food and beverages in a toilet room and any area exposed to a toxic material? 1926.51(g)

§1926.52—Occupational noise exposure.

Is protection provided against the effects of noise exposure when the sound levels exceed the permissible level of decibels based on the number of hours per day of exposure? 1926.52(a)

Have feasible administrative or engineering controls been utilized to reduce the excessive noise within permissible levels? 1926.52(b)

Is a continuing, effective hearing conservation program being administered where the sound levels are excessive? 1926.52(d)(1)

§1926.54—Nonionizing radiation.

Are only trained and qualified employees assigned to install, adjust and operate laser equipment? 1926.54(a)

Do laser operators carry proof of qualification? 1926.54(b)

Are employees who may be potentially exposed provided with antilaser eye protection? 1926.54(c)

Are placards warning of lasers posted in the laser use area? 1926.54(d)

When the laser is not required are beam shutters or caps used or is the unit turned off? 1926.54(e)

Are only mechanical or electronic means used as a detector for guiding the internal alignment of the laser? 1926.54(f)

Is the laser beam not directed at employees? 1926.54(g)

When it is raining or snowing, or when there is dust or fog in the air, is the operation of laser systems prohibited where practicable? Are employees kept out of range of the area of source and target during such weather conditions? 1926.54(h)

Does laser equipment bear a label to indicate maximum output? 1926.54(i)

Are employees not being exposed to light intensities above: direct staring: 1 microwatt per square centimeter; incidental observing: 1 milliwatt per square centimeter; diffused reflected light: 2 1/2 watts per square centimeter? 1926.54(j)

Is the laser unit in operation set up above the heads of the employees, when possible? 1926.54(k)

Are employees not being exposed to microwave power densities in excess of 10 milliwatts per square centimeter? 1926.54(l)

§1926.55—Gases, vapors, fumes, dusts, and mists.

Do employers limit an employee's exposure to any substance listed in Table 1 (Permissible Exposure Limits for Airborne Contaminants) or 2 (Mineral Dusts) of this section? 1926.55(a)

Have administrative or engineering controls been utilized to achieve compliance with paragraph? 1926.55(b)

When administrative or engineering controls are not feasible to achieve full compliance, is protective equipment or other protective measures used to keep the exposure of employees to air contaminants within the limits prescribed in this section? 1926.55(b)

§1926.56—Illumination.

Are construction areas, ramps, runways, corridors, offices, shops, and storage areas lighted to not less than the minimum illumination intensities listed in Table D-3 while any work is in progress? 1926.56 (a)

Table D-3—Minimum Illumination Intensities in Foot-Candles

Foot-candles	Area or operation
5	General construction area lighting.
3	General construction areas, concrete placement, excavation and waste areas, accessways, active storage areas, loading platforms, refueling, and field maintenance areas.
5	Indoors: warehouses, corridors, hallways, and exitways.
5	Tunnels, shafts, and general work areas: (Exception: minimum of 10 foot-candles is required at tunnel and shaft heading during drilling, mucking, and scaling. Bureau of Mines approved cap lights shall be for use in the tunnel heading.)
10	General construction plant and shops (e.g., batch plants, screening plants, mechanical and electrical equipment rooms, carpenter shops, rigging lofts and active storerooms, barracks or living quarters, locker or dressing rooms, mess halls, and indoor toilets and workrooms).
30	First aid stations, infirmaries, and offices.

§1926.57—Ventilation.

Does the employer ensure that concentrations of hazardous substances such as dusts, fumes, mists, vapors, or gases produced in the course of construction work do not exceed the limits specified in 1926.55(a)? 1926.57(a)

Are all employees working in and around open-surface tank operation instructed as to the hazards of their respective jobs, and in the personal protection and first aid procedures applicable to these hazards? 1926.57(i)(9)

§1926.59—Hazard communication.[1]

Does the employer have any hazardous materials on site? If so, does the employer have a written hazard communication program? 1910.1200(e)(1)

Does the employer have a complete list of hazardous chemicals known to be present on the worksite? 1910.1200 (e)(1)(i)

---

[1] The requirements applicable to construction work under this section are identical to those set forth at §1910.1200 of this chapter.

Does the employer have methods of informing employees of the hazards of non-routine tasks, unlabeled pipes, etc.? 1910.1200(e)(1)(ii)

Does the employer provide the other employer(s) on-site access to safety data sheets for each hazardous chemical the other employer(s)' employees may be exposed to while working? 1910 .1200(e)(2)(i)

Does the employer inform other employers of any precautionary measures they may need to take? 1910.1200 (e)(2)(ii)

Does the employer inform other employers of labeling system used in the workplace? 1910.1200(e)(2)(iii)

Are containers of hazardous chemicals, labeled, tagged, or marked? 1910.1200(f)(1)

If leaving the workplace, do labels include product identifier, signal word, hazard statement, pictogram, precautionary statement, and the name, phone number, and address of manufacturer? 1910.1200(f)(1)(i-vi)

Does the employer ensure that each container of hazardous chemicals in the workplace is labeled, tagged or marked to provide employees with the specific information regarding the physical and health hazards of chemicals? 1910.1200(f)(6)

Does the employer have an SDS for each hazardous chemical on site? 1910.1200(g)(1)

Are SDSs available to employees in their work area? 1910.1200 (g)(8)

Does the employer provide employees with effective information and training on hazardous chemicals in their work area at the time of their initial assignment, and whenever a new chemical hazard on which the employees have not been trained is introduced into their work area? 1910.1200 (h)(1)

Does employer provide employee with the following information: requirements of this section; any operation in employee's area where hazards chemicals are present; and, the location and availability of the written hazard communication program, including the required list(s) of hazardous chemicals, and safety data sheets required by this section? 1910.1200(h)(2)(i-iii)

Are employees trained at least in: methods to detect a chemical release; physical and health hazards related to chemicals on the jobsite; measures employees can take to protect themselves from these hazards; and, details of the employer's hazard communication program? 1910.1200(h)(3)(i-iv)

§1926.62—Lead.

Are employees exposed to lead at concentrations greater than 50 micrograms per cubic feet averaged over an 8-hour period? 1926.62(c)(1)

Has a determination been made as to the possibility of any employee being exposed to lead at or above the action level? 1926.62(d)(1)(i)

With respect to the tasks listed in this paragraph (d)(2)(iv), where lead is present, until the employer performs an employee exposure assessment as required in this paragraph (d) and documents that the employee performing any of the listed tasks is not exposed to lead in excess of 2,500 µg/m³ (50×PEL), does the employer treat the employee as if the employee were exposed to lead in excess of 2,500 µg/m³ and implement employee protective measures as prescribed in paragraph (d)(2)(v) of this section? 1926.62(d)(1)(iv)

Does the employer develop a written record which documents its determination that no employee is exposed to airborne concentrations of lead at or above the action level? Does this record include at least the information specified in 1926.62(d)(3)(i)? 1926.62(d)(5)

Does the employer implement engineering and work practice controls, including administrative controls, to reduce and maintain employee exposure to lead to or below the PEL to the extent that such controls are feasible? 1926.62(e)(1)

Prior to commencement of the job does each employer establish and implement a written compliance program to achieve compliance with paragraph (c) of this section? 1926.62(e)(2)(i)

For employees who use respirators required by this section, does the employer provide each employee an appropriate respirator that complies with the requirements of this paragraph? 1962(f)(1)

Does the employer provide at no cost to the employee and assure that the employee uses appropriate protective work clothing and equipment that prevents contamination of the employee and the employee's garments such as, but not limited to: overalls or similar full-body work clothing; gloves, hats, and shoes or disposable shoe coverlets; and face shields, vented goggles, or other appropriate protective equipment which complies with §1910.133 of this chapter? 1926.62(g)(1)

Area all surfaces maintained as free as practicable of accumulations of lead? 1926.62(h)(1)

Where vacuuming methods are selected, are the vacuums equipped with HEPA filters and used and emptied in a manner which minimizes the reentry of lead into the workplace? 1926.62(h)(4)

Is compressed air not used to remove lead from any surface unless the compressed air is used in conjunction with a ventilation system designed to capture the airborne dust created by the compressed air? 1926.62(h)(5)

Does the employer assure that in areas where employees are exposed to lead above the PEL without regard to the use of respirators, food or beverage is not present or consumed, tobacco products are not present or used, and cosmetics are not applied? 1926.62(i)(1)

Provide and require the use of hygiene facilities (change areas, showers and eating and hand washing facilities)? 1926.62(i)(2-5)

Does the employer make available initial medical surveillance to employees occupationally exposed on any day to lead at or above the action level? 1926.62(j)(1)(i)

Does the employer make available biological monitoring in the form of blood sampling and analysis for lead and zinc protoporphyrin levels to each employee covered under paragraphs (j)(1)(i) and (ii) of this section? 1926.62(j)(2)(i)

Does the employer ensure that each employee has access to labels on containers of lead and safety data sheets, and is trained in accordance with the provisions of HCS and paragraph (l) of this section? 1926.62(l)(1)(i)

Does the content of the employers training program include those elements addressed in 1926.62(l)(2)(i-viii)? 1926.62(l)(2)

§1926.65—Hazardous waste operations and emergency response.

Are hazardous substances and contaminated soils, liquids, and other residues handled, transported, labeled, and disposed of in accordance with this paragraph? 1926.65(j)(1)(i)

Subpart E-Personal Protective and Life Saving Equipment

§1926.95—Criteria for personal protective equipment.

Is protective equipment, including personal protective equipment for eyes, face, head, and extremities, protective clothing, respiratory devices, and protective shields and barriers, provided, used, and maintained in a sanitary and reliable condition wherever it is necessary by reason of hazards of processes or environment, chemical hazards, radiological hazards, or mechanical irritants encountered in a manner capable of causing injury or impairment? 1926.95(a)

§1926.96—Occupational foot protection.

Does safety-toe footwear for employees meet the requirements and specifications in American National Standard for Men's Safety-Toe Footwear, Z41.1-1967? 1926.96

§1926.100—Head protection.

Are protective helmets (hard hats) worn at all times where there is a possible danger of head injury from impact, falling or flying objects, or electrical shock and burns? 1926.100(a)

§1926.101—Hearing protection.

Are ear protection devices provided and used wherever it is not feasible to reduce noise levels or duration of exposures to permissible levels specified in Table D-2, Permissible Noise Exposure in 1926.52? 1926.101(a)

§1926.102—Eye and face protection.

Does the employer ensure that each affected employee uses eye and face protection when exposed to eye or face hazards from flying particles, molten metal, liquid chemicals, acids or caustic liquids, chemical gases or vapors, or potentially injurious light radiation? 1926.102(a)(1)

Is Table E-1 being used as a guide for the selection of the proper shade numbers of filter lenses or plates used in welding? 1926.102(c)(1)

Table E-1—Filter Lens Shade Numbers for Protection Against

Welding operation	Shade number
Shielded metal-arc welding 1/16-, 3/32-, 1/8-, 5/32-inch diameter electrodes	10
Gas-shielded arc welding (nonferrous) 1/16-, 3/32-, 1/8-, 5/32-inch diameter electrodes	11
Gas-shielded arc welding (ferrous) 1/16-, 3/32-, 1/8-, 5/32-inch diameter electrodes	12
Shielded metal-arc welding 3/16-, 7/32-, 1/4-inch diameter electrodes	12

Welding operation	Shade number
5/16-, 3/8-inch diameter electrodes	14
Atomic hydrogen welding	10-14
Carbon-arc welding	14
Soldering	2
Torch brazing	3 or 4
Light cutting, up to 1 inch	3 or 4
Medium cutting, 1 inch to 6 inches	4 or 5
Heavy cutting, over 6 inches	5 or 6
Gas welding (light), up to 1/8-inch	4 or 5
Gas welding (medium), 1/8-inch to 1/2-inch	5 or 6
Gas welding (heavy), over 1/2-inch	6 or 8

§1926.103—Respiratory protection.[2]

Is a respirator provided to each employee when such equipment is necessary to protect the health of such employee? 1910.134(a)(2)

§1926.106—Working over or near water.

Are employees working over or near water, where the danger of drowning exists, provided with U.S. Coast Guard-approved life jacket or buoyant work vests? 1926.106(a)

Prior to and after each use, are buoyant work vests or life preservers inspected for defects which would alter their strength or buoyancy? 1926.106(b)

Are ring buoys with at least 90 feet of line provided and readily available for emergency rescue operations? Does the distance between ring buoys not exceed 200 feet? 1926.106(c)

Is at least one lifesaving skiff immediately available at locations where employees are working over or adjacent to water? 1926.106(d)

---

[2] The requirements applicable to construction work under this section are identical to those set forth at 29 CFR 1910.134 of this chapter.

Subpart F–Fire Protection and Prevention

§1926.150—Fire protection.

Has the employer developed a fire protection program to be followed throughout all phases of the construction and demolition work? 1926.150(a)(1)

Is access to all available firefighting equipment maintained at all times 1926.150(a)(2)

Is all firefighting equipment, provided by the employer, conspicuously located? 1926.150(a)(3)

Is all firefighting equipment periodically inspected and maintained in operating condition? Is defective equipment immediately replaced? 1926.150(a)(4)

Is a fire extinguisher, rated not less than 2A, provided for each 3,000 square feet of the protected building area, or major fraction thereof, and travel distance from any point of the protected area to the nearest fire extinguisher does not exceed 100 feet? 1926.150(c)(1)(i)

Are one or more fire extinguishers, rated not less than 2A, provided on each floor? In multistory buildings, is at least one fire extinguisher located adjacent to a stairway? 1926.150(c)(1)(iv)

Is a fire extinguisher, rated not less than 10B, provided within 50 feet of wherever more than 5 gallons of flammable or combustible liquids or 5 pounds of flammable gas are being used on the jobsite? (This requirement does not apply to the integral fuel tanks of motor vehicles.) 1926.150(c)(1)(vi)

Are portable fire extinguishers inspected periodically and maintained in accordance with Maintenance and Use of Portable Fire Extinguishers, NFPA No. 10A-1970? 1926.150(c)(1)(viii)

Are fire extinguishers which have been listed or approved by a nationally recognized testing laboratory used to meet the requirements of this subpart? 1926.150(c)(1)(ix)

If the facility being constructed includes the installation of automatic sprinkler protection, does the installation closely follow the construction and is placed in service as soon as applicable laws permit following completion of each story? 1926.150(d)(1)(i)

§1926.151—Fire prevention.

Is smoking prohibited at or in the vicinity of operations which constitute a fire hazard, and is "No Smoking or Open Flame" conspicuously posted? 1926.151(a)(3)

Are temporary buildings, when located within another building or structure, of either noncombustible construction or of combustible construction having a fire resistance of not less than 1 hour? 1926.151(b)(2)

Is the entire storage site kept free from accumulation of unnecessary combustible materials? 1926.151(c)(3)

Is the method of piling solid wherever possible and in orderly and regular piles? Is no combustible material stored outdoors within 10 feet of a building or structure? 1926.151(c)(5)

Are non compatible materials, which may create a fire hazard, segregated by a barrier having a fire resistance of at least 1 hour? 1926.151(d)(3)

Is material piled to minimize the spread of fire internally and to permit convenient access for firefighting? Is stable piling maintained at all times? Is aisle space maintained to safely accommodate the widest vehicle that may be used within the building for firefighting purposes? 1926.151(d)(4)

§1926.152—Flammable liquids.

Are flammable liquids stored and handled in only approved containers and portable tanks? 1926.152(a)(1)

Are flammable liquids not stored in areas used for exits, stairways, or the safe passage of people? 1926.152(a)(2)

Is no more than 25 gallons of flammable liquid stored in a room outside of an approved storage cabinet? 1926.152(b)(1)

Is at least one portable fire extinguisher, having a rating of not less than 20-B units, located outside of, but not more than 10 feet from, the door opening into any room used for storage of more than 60 gallons of flammable liquids? 1926.152(d)(1)

Is at least one portable fire extinguisher having a rating of not less than 20-B units located not less than 25 feet, nor more than 75 feet, from any flammable liquid storage area located outside? 1926.152(d)(2)

Is drainage or another means provided to control spills? 1926.152(e)(1)

Is transfer of Category 1, 2, or 3 flammable liquids from one container to another done only when containers are electrically interconnected (bonded)? 1926.152(e)(2)

Are dispensing units protected against collision damage? 1926.152(e)(4)

Are category 1, 2, or 3 flammable liquids kept in closed containers when not actually in use? 1926.152(f)(1)

Are category 1, 2, or 3 flammable liquids used only where there are no open flames or other sources of ignition within 50 feet of the operation, unless conditions warrant greater clearance? 1926.152(f)(3)

Are flammable liquids stored in approved closed containers, in tanks located underground, or in aboveground portable tanks? 1926.152(g)(1)

Is the dispensing nozzle an approved automatic-closing type without a latch-open device? 1926.152(g)(4)

Are there no smoking or open flames in areas used for fueling, servicing fuel systems for internal combustion engines, receiving or dispensing of flammable liquids? 1926.152(g)(8)

Are conspicuous and legible signs prohibiting smoking posted? 1926.152(g)(9)

Are the motors of all equipment being fueled shut off during the fueling operation? 1926.152(g)(10)

Is at least one portable fire extinguisher with a rating of not less than 20-B:C located within 75 feet of each pump, dispenser, underground fill pipe opening and lubrication or service area? 1926.152(g)(11)

§1926.153—Liquefied petroleum gas (LP-Gas).

Are containers upright upon firm foundations or otherwise firmly secured? Is the possible effect of settling on the outlet piping guarded against by a flexible connection or special fitting? 1926.153(g)

Are portable heaters, including salamanders, equipped with an approved automatic device to shut off the flow of gas to the main burner, and pilot if used, in the event of flame failure? 1926.153(h)(8)

Is storage of LPG within buildings prohibited? 1926.153(j)

Are containers in a suitable ventilated enclosure or otherwise protected against tampering? 1926.153(k)(2)

Are storage locations provided with at least one approved portable fire extinguisher having a rating of not less than 20-B:C? 1926.153(l)

§1926.154—Temporary heating devices.

Is fresh air supplied in sufficient quantities to maintain the health and safety of workmen? Where natural means of fresh air supply is inadequate, is mechanical ventilation provided? 1926.154(a)(1)

Are temporary heating devices installed to provide clearance to combustible material not less than the amount shown in Table F-4? 1926.154(b)(1)

Table F-4

Heating appliances	Minimum clearance (inches)		
	Sides	Rear	Chimney connector
Room heater, circulating type	12	12	18
Room heater, radiant type	36	36	18

Are heaters not suitable for use on wood floors not set directly upon them or other combustible materials? When such heaters are used, do they rest on suitable heat insulating material or at least 1-inch concrete, or equivalent. Does the insulating material extend beyond the heater 2 feet or more in all directions? 1926.154(b)(3)

Are heaters used in the vicinity of combustible tarpaulins, canvas, or similar coverings located at least 10 feet from the coverings? Are the coverings securely fastened to prevent ignition or upsetting of the heater due to wind action on the covering or other material? 1926.154(b)(4)

Are heaters, when in use, set horizontally level, unless otherwise permitted by the manufacturer's markings? 1926.154(c)

Are solid fuel salamanders prohibited in buildings and on scaffolds? 1926.154(d)

Subpart G–Signs, Signals, and Barricades

§1926.200—Accident prevention signs and tags.

Are accident prevention signs and symbols visible at all times when work is being performed, and removed or covered promptly when the hazards no longer exist? 1926.200(a)

Do the design and use of all traffic control devices, including signs, signals, markings, barricades, and other devices, for protection of construction workers conform with Part 6 of the MUTCD? 1926.200(g)(2)

§1926.201—Signaling.

Do signaling by flaggers and the use of flaggers, including warning garments worn by flaggers, conform to Part 6 of the MUTCD? 1926.201(a)

Subpart H-Materials Handling, Storage, Use, and Disposal

§1926.250—General requirements for storage.

Are all materials stored in tiers either stacked, racked, blocked, interlocked, or otherwise secured to prevent sliding, falling, or collapse? 1926.250(a)(1)

Does the weight of stored materials on floors within buildings and structures not exceed the maximum safe load limits? 1926.250(a)(2)(i)

Are aisles and passageways kept clear and in good repair to provide for the free and safe movement of material handling equipment or employees? 1926.250(a)(3)

Is material stored inside buildings under construction placed more than 6 feet from any hoistway or inside floor openings, and more than 10 feet from any exterior wall which does not extend above the top of the stored material? 1926.250(b)(1)

Are materials stored on scaffolds or runways not in excess of supplies needed for immediate operations? 1926.250(b)(5)

Does used lumber have all nails withdrawn before stacking? 1926.250(b)(8)(i)

Are storage areas kept free from accumulation of materials that constitute hazards from tripping, fire, explosion, or pest harborage? 1926.250(c)

§1926.251—Rigging equipment for material handling.

Is all rigging equipment for material handling inspected prior to use on each shift and as necessary during its use to ensure that it is safe? 1926.251(a)(1)

Do employers ensure that rigging equipment is not used without affixed, legible identification markings, required by paragraph (a)(2)(i) of this section? 1926.251(a)(2)(iii)

Each day before being used, are the sling and all fastenings and attachments inspected for damage or defects by a competent person designated by the employer? Are additional inspections performed during sling use, where service conditions warrant? Are damaged or defective slings immediately removed from service? 1926.251(a)(6)

Do alloy steel chain slings have a permanently affixed durable identification stating size, grade, rated capacity, and manufacturer? 1926.251(b)(1)

Do hooks, rings, oblong links, pear-shaped links, welded or mechanical coupling links, and other attachments, when used with alloy steel chains, have a rated capacity at least equal to that of the chain? 1926.251(b)(2)

Does the employer make, maintain, and make available for examination a record of the most recent month that each alloy steel chain sling was inspected? 1926.251(b)(6)(ii)

When U-bolt wire rope clips are used to form eyes, are clips properly spaced and installed? 1926.251(c)(5) and (c)(5)(i)

§1926.252—Disposal of waste materials.

Whenever materials are dropped more than 20 feet to any point lying outside the exterior walls of the building, is an enclosed chute of wood, or equivalent material, used? 1926.252(a)

When debris is dropped through holes in the floor without the use of chutes, is the area onto which the material is dropped completely enclosed with barricades not less than 42 inches high and not less than 6 feet back from the projected edge of the opening above? Are signs warning of the hazard of falling materials posted at each level? Is removal not permitted in this lower area until debris handling ceases above? 1926.252(b)

Are all scrap lumber, waste material, and rubbish removed from the immediate work area as the work progresses? 1926.252(c)

Does disposal of waste material or debris by burning comply with local fire regulations? 1926.252(d)

Are all solvent waste, oily rags, and flammable liquids kept in fire-resistant covered containers until removed from worksite? 1926.252(e)

Subpart I-Tools-Hand and Power

§1926.300—General requirements.

Are hand and power tools furnished by employer or employee maintained in a safe condition? 1926.300(a)

When power operated tools are designed to accommodate guards, are they equipped with such guards when in use? 1926.300(b)(1)

Are power tools, belts, gears, shafts, pulleys, sprockets, spindles, drums, fly wheels, chains, and other reciprocating, rotating or moving parts of equipment properly guarded? 1926.300(b)(2)

Does abrasive wheel machinery have tongues properly adjusted, never exceeding ¼ inch? 1926.300(b)(7)

Are employees using hand and power tools and exposed to the hazard of falling, flying, abrasive, and splashing objects, or exposed to harmful dusts, fumes, mists, vapors, or gases provided with the particular personal protective equipment necessary to protect them from the hazard? 1926.300(c)

§1926.301—Hand tools.

Do employers not issue nor permit the use of unsafe hand tools? 1926.301(a)

Are impact tools free of mushroomed heads? 1926.301(c)

Are wooden tool handles free of splinters and cracks? 1926.301(d)

§1926.302—Power-operated hand tools.

Are electric power operated tools equipped with proper ground or are they double-insulated? 1926.302(a)(1)

Is the use of electric cords for hoisting or lowering tools not permitted? 1926.302(a)(2)

Is the hose or whip secured to the pneumatic tool by some positive means to prevent the tool from becoming accidentally disconnected? 1926.302(b)(1)

Are safety clips and retainers securely installed and maintained on pneumatic impact tools to prevent attachments from being accidentally expelled? 1926.302(b)(2)

Do all pneumatically driven nailers, staplers, and other similar equipment provided with automatic fastener feed, which operate at more than 100 psi pressure at the tool, have a safety device on the muzzle to prevent the tool from ejecting fasteners, unless the muzzle is in contact with the work surface? 1926.302(b)(3)

When compressed air is used for cleaning purposes is nozzle pressure reduced to less than 30 psi? 1926.302(b)(4)

Is the manufacturer's safe operating pressure for hoses, pipes, valves, filters, and other fittings not exceeded? 1926.302(b)(5)

Is the use of hoses for hoisting or lowering tools not permitted? 1926.302(b)(6)

Do all hoses exceeding 1/2-inch inside diameter have a safety device at the source of supply or branch line to reduce pressure in case of hose failure? 1926.302(b)(7)

Are all fuel powered tools stopped while being refueled, serviced, or maintained, and is fuel transported, handled, and stored in accordance with subpart F of this part? 1926.302(c)(1)

Have all employees who operate powder-actuated tools been trained in the use of the particular tool they use? 1926.302(e)(1)

Are powder-actuated tools inspected each day before loading to see that safety devices are in proper working condition? 1926.302(e)(2)

Are powder-actuated tools left unloaded until they are ready for immediate use? Are neither loaded nor empty tools pointed at any employees? Are hands kept clear of the open barrel end? 1926.302(e)(5)

Are loaded tools not left unattended? 1926.302(e)(6)

Are fasteners not be driven into very hard or brittle materials including, but not limited to, cast iron, glazed tile, surface-hardened steel, glass block, live rock, face brick, or hollow tile? 1926.302(e)(7)

Is driving into materials, which are easily penetrated, avoided unless such materials are backed by a substance that will prevent the pin or fastener from passing completely through and creating a flying missile hazard on the other side? 1926.302(e)(8)

Is no fastener driven into a spalled area caused by an unsatisfactory fastening? 1926.302(e)(9)

Are tools not be used in an explosive or flammable atmosphere? 1926.302(e)(10)

Are all tools used with the correct shield, guard, or attachments recommended by the manufacturer? 1926.302(e)(11)

Do powder-actuated tools used by employees meet all other applicable requirements of ANSI, A10.3-1970, Safety Requirements for Explosive-Actuated Fastening Tools? 1926.302(e)(12)

§1926.303—Abrasive wheels and tools.

Are grinding machines equipped with safety guards? 1926.303(b)(1)

Are abrasive wheel grinders provided with safety guards which cover the spindle ends, nut, and flange projections? 1926.303(b)(2)

Are all abrasive wheels closely inspected and ring-tested before mounting to ensure they are free from cracks or defects? 1926.303(c)(7)

Do offhand grinding machines have work rests properly adjusted within 1/8 inch to the wheel to prevent work from being jammed in the opening? 1926.303(e)

§1926.304—Woodworking tools.

Do all portable circular saws have a guard above the base plate, and a guard below the base plate, which will automatically and instantly return to the covering position when the saw is withdrawn from the work? 1926.304(d)

Do all radial saws have upper and lower blade guards? 1926.304(g)(1)

Do circular hand-fed rip saws have an upper blade guard? 1926.304(i)(1)

§1926.305—Jacks-lever and ratchet, screw, and hydraulic.

Is the manufacturer's rated capacity legibly marked on all jacks and not be exceeded? 1926.305(a)(1)

After the load has been raised, is it cribbed, blocked, or otherwise secured at once? 1926.305(d)(1)(i)

§1926.306—Air receivers.

Is every air receiver equipped with an indicating pressure gage (so located as to be readily visible) and with one or more spring-loaded safety valves? Does the total relieving capacity of safety valves prevent the pressure in the receiver from exceeding the maximum allowable working pressure by more than 10 percent? 1926.306(b)(3)(i)

Subpart J-Welding and Cutting

§1926.350—Gas welding and cutting.

When transporting, moving, or storing compressed gas cylinders, are cap cylinders in place and secured? 1926.350(a)(1)

Are cylinders secured in a vertical position when transported by powered vehicles? 1926.350(a)(4)

Are the cylinder valves closed when work is finished, cylinders are empty, and cylinders are moved? 1926.350(a)(8)

Are compressed gas cylinders secured in an upright position at all times? 1926.350(a)(9)

Are oxygen cylinders in storage separated from fuel-gas cylinders or combustible materials (especially oil or grease) by a minimum distance of 20 feet or a noncombustible barrier at least 5 feet high having a fire-resistance rating of at least one-half hour? 1926.350(a)(10)

Are cylinders, full or empty, never used as rollers or supports? 1926.350(c)(1)

Are employees instructed in the safe use of fuel gas? 1926.350(d)

If, when the valve on a fuel gas cylinder is opened, there is found to be a leak around the valve stem, is the valve closed and the gland nut tightened? If this action does not stop the leak, is the use of the cylinder discontinued, and properly tagged and removed from the work area? In the event that fuel gas should leak from the cylinder valve, rather than from the valve stem, and the gas cannot be shut off, is the cylinder properly tagged and removed from the work area? 1926.350(d)(5)

Are all hose in use, carrying acetylene, oxygen, natural or manufactured fuel gas, or any gas or substance which may ignite or enter into combustion, or be in any way harmful to employees, inspected at the beginning of each working shift? 1926.350(f)(3)

Are torches inspected for leaking shut off valves, hose couplings, and tip connections at the beginning of each work shift? 1926.350(g)(2)

Are oxygen and fuel gas regulators in proper working order? 1926.350(h)

Are oxygen cylinders and fittings kept away from oil and grease? 1926.350(i)

§1926.351—Arc welding and cutting.

Are only manual electrode holders, which are specifically designed for arc welding and cutting, and are of a capacity capable of safely handling the maximum rated current required by the electrodes, used? 1926.351(a)(1)

Are any current-carrying parts passing through the portion of the holder, which the arc welder or cutter grips in his hand, and the outer surfaces of the jaws of the holder, fully insulated against the maximum voltage encountered to ground? 1926.351(a)(2)

Are all arc welding and cutting cables of the completely insulated, flexible type, capable of handling the maximum current requirements of the work in progress, taking into account the duty cycle under which the arc welder or cutter is working? 1926.351(b)(1)

Is only cable, free from repair or splices for a minimum distance of 10 feet from the cable end to which the electrode holder is connected, used; or do cables have standard insulated connectors or splices whose insulating quality is equal to that of the cable? 1926.351(b)(2)

When it becomes necessary to connect or splice lengths of cable one to another, are substantial insulated connectors of a capacity at least equivalent to that of the cable being used? If connections are effected by means of cable lugs, are they securely fastened together to give good electrical contact, and are the exposed metal parts of the lugs completely insulated? 1926.351(b)(3)

Are cables in need of repair not used? When a cable, other than the cable lead referred to in paragraph (b)(2) of this section, becomes worn to the extent of exposing bare conductors, is the exposed portion protected by means of rubber and friction tape or other equivalent insulation? 1926.351(b)(4)

Does a ground return cable have a safe current carrying capacity equal to or exceeding the specified maximum output capacity of the arc welding or cutting unit which it services? When a single ground return cable services more than one unit, does its safe current-carrying capacity equal or exceed the total specified maximum output capacities of all the units which it services? 1926.351(c)(1)

Are pipelines containing gases or flammable liquids, or conduits containing electrical circuits, not used as a ground return? 1926.351(c)(2)

When a structure or pipeline is employed as a ground return circuit, is it determined that the required electrical contact exists at all joints? Does the generation of an arc, sparks, or heat at any point cause rejection of the structures as a ground circuit? 1926.351(c)(3)

When a structure or pipeline is continuously employed as a ground return circuit, are all joints bonded, and are periodic inspections conducted to ensure that no condition of electrolysis or fire hazard exists? 1926.351(c)(4)

Are frames of all arc welding and cutting machines grounded? 1926.351(c)(5)

Are all ground connections inspected to ensure that they are mechanically strong and electrically adequate for the required current? 1926.351(c)(6)

Are employees instructed in the safe means of arc welding and cutting? 1926.351(d)

Are electrodes removed and electrode holders placed or protected so they cannot make electrical contact with employees or conducting objects when the holders are left unattended? 1926.351(d)(1)

Are welding and cutting operations shielded by noncombustible or flameproof screens whenever practicable? 1926.351(e)

§1926.352—Fire prevention.

If the object to be welded, cut, or heated cannot be moved and if all the fire hazards cannot be removed, are positive means taken to confine the heat, sparks, and slag, and to protect the immovable fire hazards from them? 1926.352(b)

Is suitable fire extinguishing equipment immediately available in the work area and ready for instant use? 1926.352(d)

When the welding, cutting, or heating operation is such that normal fire prevention precautions are not sufficient, is additional personnel assigned to guard against fire while the actual welding, cutting, or heating operation is being performed, and for a sufficient period of time after completion of the work to ensure that no possibility of fire exists? Is such personnel instructed as to the specific anticipated fire hazards and how the provided firefighting equipment is to be used? 1926.352(e)

Are drums, containers, or hollow structures which have contained toxic or flammable substances either filled with water or thoroughly cleaned of such substances, ventilated and tested before welding, cutting, or heating is undertaken on them? 1926.352(i)

Before heat is applied to a drum, container, or hollow structure, is a vent or opening provided to release built up pressure? 1926.352(j)

§1926.353—Ventilation and protection in welding, cutting, and heating.

Is mechanical ventilation system of sufficient capacity and so arranged to remove fumes and smoke and keep the concentration within safe limits? 1926.353(a)(2-3)

When employees are welding, cutting, or heating in confined spaces, is either general mechanical ventilation or local exhaust ventilation provided; or when sufficient ventilation cannot be obtained without blocking the means of access, are employees protected with airline respirators and an employee on the outside of the confined space assigned to maintain communication with them? 1926.353(b)(1-2)

Are employees who are performing any type of welding, cutting, or heating protected by suitable eye protective equipment? 1926.353(e)(2)

Subpart K-Electrical

§1926.403—General requirements.

Does the employer ensure that electrical equipment is free from recognized hazards that are likely to cause death or serious physical harm to employees? 1926.403(b)(1)

Is equipment being installed and used in accordance with the instructions included in its listing, labeling, or certification? 1926.403(b)(2)

Is electric equipment firmly secured to the surface on which it is mounted? 1926.403(d)(1)

Are disconnecting means for motors and appliances legibly marked to indicate its purpose unless located and arranged so the purpose is evident? Is each service, feeder, and branch circuit, at its disconnecting means or overcurrent device, legibly marked to indicate its purpose, unless located and arranged so the purpose is evident? 1926.403(h)

Is sufficient access and working space provided and maintained about all electric equipment to permit ready and safe operation and maintenance of such equipment? 1926.403(i)(1)

Are live electrical parts operating at 50 volts or more guarded against accidental contact? 1926.403(i)(2)(i)

Are entrances to rooms and other guarded locations containing exposed live parts marked with conspicuous warning signs forbidding unqualified persons to enter? 1926.403(i)(2)(iii)

If equipment is exposed to physical damage from vehicular traffic, are guards provided to prevent such damage? 1926.403(j)(2)(ii)

Where energized parts are exposed, is the minimum clear workspace at least 6 feet 6 inches high (measured vertically from the floor or platform), or at least 3 feet (914 mm) wide (measured parallel to the equipment)? 1926.403(j)(3)

§1926.404—Wiring design and protection.

Is the polarity of conductors correct? 1926.404(a)(2)

Are GFCIs or an assured equipment grounding program used to protect employees? 1926.404(b)(1)(i)

Are all 120-volt, single phase, 15- and 20-ampere receptacle outlets on construction sites, which are not a part of the permanent wiring of the building or structure and which are in use by employees, protected by GFCIs? 1926.404(b)(1)(ii)

Do outlet devices have an ampere rating not less than the load to be served? 1926.404(b)(2)

Table K-4—Receptacle Ratings for Various Size Circuits

Circuit rating amperes	Receptacle rating amperes
15	Not over 15.
20	15 or 20.
30	30.
40	40 or 50.
50	50.

Are signs warning of high voltage posted where unauthorized employees might come in contact with live parts? 1926.404(d)(2)(ii)

Is the path to ground from circuits, equipment, and enclosures permanent and continuous? 1926.404(f)(6)

Are exposed noncurrent-carrying metal parts of cord- and plug-connected equipment which may become energized grounded? 1926.404(f)(7)(iv)

§1926.405—Wiring methods, components, and equipment for general use.

Are all lamps for general illumination protected from accidental contact or breakage? 1926.405(a)(2)(ii)(E)

Are temporary lights not suspended by their electric cords unless cords and lights are designed for this means of suspension? 1926.405(a)(2)(ii)(F)

Are flexible cords and cables protected from damage? 1926.405(a)(2)(ii)(I)

Are extension cord sets used with portable electric tools and appliances of three-wire type and designed for hard or extra-hard usage? Are flexible cords used with temporary and portable lights designed for hard or extra-hard usage? 1926.405(a)(2)(ii)(J)

Are conductors entering boxes, cabinets, or fittings protected from abrasion and are unused openings in cabinets, boxes, and fittings closed? 1926.405(b)(1)

Are all pull boxes, junction boxes, and fittings provided with covers? 1926.405(b)(2)

Are cabinets, cut out boxes, fittings, boxes, and panel board enclosures in damp locations installed so as to prevent moisture from entering the enclosures, and in wet locations enclosed in weatherproof enclosures? 1926.405(e)(1)

Are switches, circuit breakers, and switchboards in damp locations installed in wet locations enclosed in weatherproof enclosures? 1926.405(e)(2)

Are flexible cords and cables not used as a substitute for fixed wiring of a structure; do not run through holes in walls, ceilings, or floors; do not run through doorways or windows without protection provided to avoid damage; not attached to building surfaces; and not concealed behind walls, ceilings, or floors? 1926.405(g)(1)(iii)(A-E)

Are flexible cords only used in continuous lengths without splice or tap? If repaired, are hard service flexible cords No. 12 or larger spliced so that the splice retains the insulation, outer sheath properties, and usage characteristics of the cord? 1926.405(g)(2)(iii)

Are flexible cords connected to devices and fittings so that strain relief is provided which will prevent pull from being directly transmitted to joints or terminal screws? 1926.405(g)(2)(iv)

Are fixtures and receptacles in wet or damp locations identified for that purpose and installed so that water cannot enter or accumulate? 1926.405(j)(1)(v)

§1926.407—Hazardous (classified) locations.

Is all electrical equipment, wiring methods, and installations used in hazardous locations either approved for the location or as intrinsically safe? 1926.407(b)

§1926.416—General requirements.

Does the employer prohibit an employee from working in such proximity to any part of an electric power circuit that the employee could contact the electric power circuit in the course of work, unless the employee is protected against electric shock by deenergizing the circuit and grounding it or by guarding it effectively by insulation or other means? 1926.416(a)(1)

Does the employer post and maintain proper warning signs where a person, tool, or machine may come into contact with any part of an energized electric power circuit? 1926.416(a)(3)

Are working spaces, walkways, and similar locations clear of cords so as not to create a hazard to employees? 1926.416(b)(2)

Are worn or frayed electric cords or cables not used? 1926.416(e)(1)

Are extension cords not be fastened with staples, hung from nails, or suspended by wire? 1926.416(e)(2)

§1926.417—Lockout and tagging of circuits.

Are equipment or circuits that are deenergized rendered inoperative and have tags attached at all points where such equipment or circuits can be energized? 1926.417(b)

Subpart L—Scaffolds

§1926.451—General requirements.

Are scaffolds and scaffold components capable of supporting, without failure, its own weight and at least 4 times the maximum intended load applied or transmitted to it? 1926.451(a)

Are scaffold platforms fully planked? 1926.451(b)(1)

Except as provided in paragraphs (b)(3) (i) and (ii) of this section, are the front edge of all platforms not more than 14 inches from the face of the work, unless guardrail systems are erected along the front edge and/or personal fall arrest systems are used in accordance with paragraph (g) of this section to protect employees from falling? 1926.451(b)(3)

Is the maximum distance from the face for outrigger scaffolds 3 inches? 1926.451(b)(3)(i)

Is the maximum distance from the face for plastering and lathing operations 18 inches? 1926.451(b)(3)(ii)

Unless cleated or otherwise restrained by hooks or equivalent means does each end of a platform extend over the centerline of its support at least 6 inches and no more than 12 inches? 1926.451(b)(4) & (b)(5)(i)

Are scaffold components manufactured by different manufacturers not intermixed unless the components fit together without force and the scaffold's structural integrity is maintained by the user? 1926.451(b)(10)

Are scaffold components manufactured by different manufacturers not modified in order to intermix them unless a competent person determines the resulting scaffold is structurally sound? 1926.451(b)(10)

Are supported scaffolds with a height to base width ratio of more than four to one restrained from tipping by guying, tying, bracing, or equivalent means? 1926.451(c)(1)

Are guys, ties, and braces installed according to the scaffold manufacturer's recommendations, or at the closest horizontal member to the 4:1 height and be repeated vertically at locations of horizontal members every 20 feet or less thereafter for scaffolds 3 feet wide or less, and every 26 feet or less thereafter for scaffolds greater than 3 feet wide? 1926.451(c)(1)(ii)

Do supported scaffold poles, legs, posts, frames, and uprights bear on base plates and mud sills or other adequate firm foundation? 1926.451(c)(2)

Are footings level, sound, rigid, and capable of supporting the loaded scaffold without settling or displacement? 1926.451(c)(2)(i)

Are fork-lifts not used to support scaffold platforms unless the entire platform is attached to the fork and the fork-lift is not moved horizontally while the platform is occupied? 1926.451(c)(2)(v)

Are poles, legs, posts, frames, and uprights in supported scaffolds plumb and braced to prevent swaying and displacement? 1926.451(c)(3)

Are all suspension scaffold support devices, such as outrigger beams, cornice hooks, parapet clamps, and similar devices, resting on surfaces capable of supporting at least 4 times the load imposed on them by the scaffold operating at the rated load of the hoist (or at least 1.5 times the load imposed on them by the scaffold at the stall capacity of the hoist, whichever is greater)? 1926.451(d)(1)

Are suspension scaffold outrigger beams made of structural metal or equivalent strength material, and restrained to prevent movement? 1926.451(d)(2)

Are the inboard ends of suspension scaffold outrigger beams stabilized by bolts or other direct connections to the floor or roof deck; or do they have their inboard ends stabilized by counterweights, excluding masons' multi-point adjustable suspension scaffold outrigger beams)? 1926.451(d)(3)

Before the scaffold is used, are direct connections evaluated by a competent person who confirms, based on the evaluation, that the supporting surfaces are capable of supporting the loads to be imposed? 1926.451(d)(3)(i)

Are only those items specifically designed as counterweights used to counterweight scaffold systems? 1926.451(d)(3)(iii)

Are counterweights secured by mechanical means to the outrigger beams to prevent accidental displacement? 1926.451(d)(3)(iv)

Are outrigger beams which are not stabilized by bolts or other direct connections to the floor or roof deck, secured by tiebacks? 1926.451(d)(3)(vi)

Are outrigger beams placed perpendicular to its bearing support, usually the face of the building or structure, where possible? Where not possible, is the outrigger beam placed at some other angle, provided opposing angle tiebacks are used? 1926.451(d)(3)(viii)

Are tiebacks secured to a structurally sound anchorage on the building or structure? 1926.451(d)(3)(ix)

Are tiebacks installed perpendicular to the face of the building or structure, or are opposing angle tiebacks installed? 1926.451(d)(3)(x)

When an outrigger beam is used, is the shackle or clevis with which the rope is attached to the outrigger beam placed directly over the center line of the stirrup? 1926.451(d)(4)(v)

Are suspension scaffold support devices such as cornice hooks, roof hooks, roof irons, parapet clamps, or similar devices made of steel, wrought iron, or materials of equivalent strength? 1926.451(d)(5)(i)

Are suspension scaffold support devices supported by bearing blocks? 1926.451(d)(5)(ii)

Are suspension scaffold support devices secured against movement by tiebacks installed at right angles to the face of the building or structure, or are opposing angle tiebacks installed and secured to a structurally sound point of anchorage on the building or structure? 1926.451(d)(5)(iii)

(202)

When winding drum hoists are used on a suspension scaffold, do they contain at least four wraps of the suspension rope at the lowest point of scaffold travel? 1926.451(d)(6)

Is the use of repaired wire rope as suspension rope prohibited? 1926.451(d)(7)

Are ropes inspected for defects by a competent person prior to each workshift and after every occurrence which could affect a rope's integrity? 1926.451(d)(10)

When wire rope clips are used on suspension scaffolds, is there a minimum of 3 wire rope clips installed, with the clips a minimum of 6 rope diameters apart? 1926.451(d)(12)(i)

When wire rope clips are used on suspension scaffolds, are clips installed according to the manufacturer's recommendations? 1926.451(d)(12)(ii)

Are gears and brakes of power-operated hoists used on suspension scaffolds enclosed? 1926.451(d)(15)

In addition to the normal operating brake, do suspension scaffold power-operated hoists and manually operated hoists have a braking device or locking pawl which engages automatically when a hoist makes either of the following uncontrolled movements: an instantaneous change in momentum or an accelerated overspeed? 1926.451(d)(16)

Do manually operated hoists require a positive crank force to descend? 1926.451(d)(17)

Are two-point and multi-point suspension scaffolds tied or otherwise secured to prevent them from swaying, as determined to be necessary by a competent person? 1926.451(d)(18)

Are devices *whose sole function* is to provide emergency escape and rescue not used as working platforms? This provision does not preclude the use of systems which are designed to function both as suspension scaffolds and emergency systems. 1926.451(d)(19)

Is safe access to scaffold platforms provided to employees working on scaffolds, and no crossbraces are used as a means of access? 1926.451(e)(1)

Are hook-on and attachable ladders positioned so that their bottom rung is not more that 24 inches above the scaffold supporting level? 1926.451(e)(2)(ii)

When hook-on and attachable ladders are used on a supported scaffold more than 35 feet high, do they have rest platforms at 35-foot maximum vertical intervals? 1926.451(e)(2)(iii)

Are stairtowers (scaffold stairway/towers) positioned such that their bottom step is not more than 24 inches above the scaffold supporting level? 1926.451(e)(4)

Is a stairrail consisting of a toprail and a midrail provided on each side of each scaffold stairway? 1926.451(e)(4)(i)

Do handrails, and toprails that serve as handrails, provide an adequate handhold for employees grasping them to avoid falling? 1926.451(e)(4)(iii)

Are stairrail systems and handrails surfaced to prevent injury to employees from punctures or lacerations, and to prevent snagging of clothing? 1926.451(e)(4)(iv)

Are the ends of stairrail systems and handrails constructed so that they do not constitute a projection hazard? 1926.451(e)(4)(v)

Are handrails, and toprails that are used as handrails, at least 3 inches from other objects? 1926.451(e)(4)(vi)

Are stairrails not less than 28 inches nor more than 37 inches from the upper surface of the stairrail to the surface of the tread, in line with the face of the riser at the forward edge of the tread? 1926.451(e)(4)(vii)

Is a landing platform at least 18 inches wide by at least 18 inches long provided at each level? 1926.451(e)(4)(viii)

Is each scaffold stairway at least 18 inches wide between stairrails? 1926.451(e)(4)(ix)

Do treads and landings have slip-resistant surfaces? 1926.451(e)(4)(x)

Is riser height uniform, within 1/4 inch, for each flight of stairs? 1926.451(e)(4)(xiii)

Is tread depth uniform, within 1/4 inch, for each flight of stairs? 1926.451(e)(4)(xiv)

Are scaffolds and scaffold components not loaded in excess of their maximum intended loads or rated capacities, whichever is less? 1926.451(f)(1)

Are scaffolds inspected for visible defects by a competent person before each work shift, and after any occurrence which could affect a scaffold's structural integrity? 1926.451(f)(3)

Is any part of a scaffold damaged or weakened, such that its strength is less than that required by paragraph (a) of this section, immediately repaired or replaced, braced to meet those provisions, or removed from service until repaired? 1926.451(f)(4)

Are scaffolds not moved horizontally while employees are on them, unless they have been designed by a registered professional engineer specifically for such movement or, for mobile scaffolds, where the provisions of §1926.452(w) are followed? 1926.451(f)(5)

Is the clearance between scaffolds and power lines as follows? Are scaffolds not erected, used, dismantled, altered, or moved such that they or any conductive material handled on them might come closer to exposed and energized power lines than as follows? 1926.451(f)(6)

Insulated lines voltage	Minimum distance	Alternatives
Less than 300 volts	3 feet	
300 volts to 50 kv	10 feet	
More than 50 kv	10 feet plus 0.4 inches for each 1 kv over 50 kv	2 times the length of the line insulator, but never less than 10 feet.

Uninsulated lines voltage	Minimum distance	Alternatives
Less than 50 kv	10 feet	
More than 50 kv	10 feet plus 0.4 inches for each 1 kv over 50 kv	2 times the length of the line insulator, but never less than 10 feet.

Are scaffolds erected, moved, dismantled, or altered only under the supervision and direction of a competent person qualified in scaffold erection, moving, dismantling or alteration? 1926.451(f)(7)

Are employees prohibited from working on scaffolds covered with snow, ice, or other slippery material except as necessary for removal of such materials? 1926.451(f)(8)

Is debris not allowed to accumulate on platforms? 1926.451(f)(13)

Are makeshift devices, such as but not limited to boxes and barrels, not used on top of scaffold platforms to increase the working level height of employees? 1926.451(f)(14)

Are employees who on a scaffold more than 10 feet above a lower level protected from falling to that lower level? 1926.451(g)(1)

When vertical lifelines are used, are they fastened to a fixed safe point of anchorage, independent of the scaffold, and protected from sharp edges and abrasion? 1926.451(g)(3)(i)

Are guardrail systems installed along all open sides and ends of platforms? 1926.451(g)(4)(i)

Is the top edge height of toprails or equivalent member on supported scaffolds manufactured or placed in service after January 1, 2000, installed between 38 and 45 inches above the platform surface? Is the top edge height on supported scaffolds manufactured and placed in service before January 1, 2000, and on all suspended scaffolds where both a guardrail and a personal fall arrest system are required, between 36 inches and 45 inches? When conditions warrant, does the height of the top edge exceed the 45-inch height, and the guardrail system meets all other criteria of paragraph (g)(4)? 1926.451(g)(4)(ii)

When midrails, screens, mesh, intermediate vertical members, solid panels, or equivalent structural members are used, are they installed between the top edge of the guardrail system and the scaffold platform? 1926.451(g)(4)(iii)

If crossbracing is used in place of a midrail, is the crossing point of two braces between 20 inches and 30 inches above the work platform? Or if used as a toprail, is the crossing point of two braces between 38 inches and 48 inches above the work platform? Are the end points at each upright no more than 48 inches apart? 1926.451(g)(4)(xv)

In addition to wearing hard-hats, are employees provided with additional protection from falling hand tools, debris, and other small objects through the installation of toeboards, screens, or guardrail systems, or through the erection of debris nets, catch platforms or canopy structures that contain or deflect the falling objects? 1926.451(h)(1)

Is a toeboard erected along the edge of platforms more than 10 feet above lower levels for a distance sufficient to protect employees below, except on float (ship) scaffolds where an edging of ¾ × 1 ½ inch wood or equivalent is used in lieu of toeboards? 1926.451(h)(2)(ii)

Are toeboards at least 3 ½ inches high from the top edge of the toeboard to the level of the walking/working surface; securely fastened in place at the outermost edge of the platform; and have not more than ¼ inch clearance above the walking/working surface? 1926.451(h)(4)(ii)

§1926.452—Additional requirements applicable to specific types of scaffolds.

In addition to the applicable requirements of 1926.451, has the employer addressed any additional requirements which are applicable to specific types of scaffolds? 1926.452(a-y)

Is the scaffold positioned so that swinging cannot bring the scaffold into contact with another surface? 1926.452(o)(2)(iv)

Are scaffolds plumb, level, and squared? 1926.452(w)(1)

Are scaffold casters and wheels locked with positive wheel and/or wheel and swivel locks, or equivalent means, to prevent movement of the scaffold while the scaffold is used in a stationary manner? 1926.452(w)(2)

Are scaffolds stabilized to prevent tipping during movement? 1926.452(w)(5)

Is the surface on which the scaffold is being moved within 3 degrees of level, and free of pits, holes, and obstructions? 1926.452(w)(6)(i)

Are employees not allowed on any part of the mobile scaffold which extends outward beyond the wheels, casters, or other supports? 1926.452(w)(6)(v)

Do platforms not extend outward beyond the base supports of the scaffold unless outrigger frames or equivalent devices are used to ensure stability? 1926.452(w)(7)

Are caster stems and wheel stems pinned or otherwise secured in scaffold legs or adjustment screws? 1926.452(w)(9)

Does an employee wear stilts on a scaffold only if it is a large area scaffold? 1926.452(y)(1)

When an employee is using stilts on a large area scaffold where a guardrail system is used to provide fall protection, is the guardrail system increased in height by an amount equal to the height of the stilts being used by the employee? 1926.452(y)(2)

Are surfaces on which stilts are used flat and free of pits, holes and obstructions, such as debris, as well as other tripping and falling hazards? 1926.452(y)(3)

Are stilts properly maintained? Is any alteration of the original equipment approved by the manufacturer? 1926.452(y)(4)

§1926.453—Aerial lifts.

Are aerial lifts designed and constructed in conformance with the applicable requirements of American National Standards for "Vehicle Mounted Elevating and Rotating Work Platforms," ANSI A92.2-1969, including appendix? 1926.453(a)(1)

Are lift controls tested each day prior to use to determine that such controls are in safe working condition? 1926.453(b)(2)(i)

Do only authorized persons operate an aerial lift? 1926.453(b)(2)(ii)

Is belting off to an adjacent pole, structure, or equipment while working from an aerial lift not permitted? 1926.453(b)(2)(iii)

Do employees always stand firmly on the floor of the basket, and do not sit or climb on the edge of the basket or use planks, ladders, or other devices for a work position? 1926.453(b)(2)(iv)

Is a body belt worn and a lanyard attached to the boom or basket when working from an aerial lift? 1926.453(b)(2)(v)

Are boom and basket load limits specified by the manufacturer not exceeded? 1926.453(b)(2)(vi)

Is the aerial lift truck stationary when the boom is elevated in a working position with men in the basket, except for equipment which is specifically designed for this type of operation in accordance with the provisions of paragraphs (a) (1) and (2) of this section? 1926.453(b)(2)(viii)

Do articulating boom and extensible boom platforms, primarily designed as personnel carriers, have both platform (upper) and lower controls? Are upper controls in or beside the platform within easy reach of the operator? Do lower controls provide for overriding the upper controls? Are controls plainly marked as to their function? Are lower level controls not operated unless permission has been obtained from the employee in the lift, except in case of emergency? 1926.453(b)(2)(ix)

§1926.454—Training requirements.

Are employees who perform work while on a scaffold trained by a person qualified in the subject matter to recognize the hazards associated with the type of scaffold being used and to understand the procedures to control or minimize those hazards? 1926.454(a)

Does the training address the nature of electrical hazards; fall hazards; falling object hazards; procedures for dealing with electrical hazards; for erecting, maintaining, and disassembling fall protection systems; falling object protection systems; proper use of the scaffold and proper handling of materials on the scaffold; maximum intended load and load carrying capacities of scaffolds used in the work area? 1926.454(a)(1-4)

Are employees involved in erecting, disassembling, moving, operating, repairing, maintaining, or inspecting a scaffold trained by a competent person? 1926.454(b)

Are employees retrained where there is reason to believe that an employee lacks the skill or understanding needed for safe work involving the erection, use, or dismantling of scaffolds? 1926.454(c)

Subpart M–Fall Protection

§1926.501—Duty to have fall protection.

Does the employer determine if the walking/working surfaces on which its employees are to work have the strength and structural integrity to support employees safely? 1926.501(a)(2)

Are employees on a walking/working surface with an unprotected side or edge which is 6 feet or more above a lower level protected from falling by the use of guardrail systems, safety net systems, or PFAS? 1926.501(b)(1)

Are employees who are constructing a leading edge 6 feet or more above lower levels protected from falling by guardrail systems, safety net systems, or PFAS? (Exception: When the employer can demonstrate that it is infeasible or creates a greater hazard to use these systems, does the employer develop and implement a fall protection plan which meets the requirements of paragraph (k) of §1926.502?) 1926.501(b)(2)(i)

Is each employee in a hoist area protected from falling 6 feet or more to lower levels by guardrail systems or PFAS? 1926.501(b)(3)

In hoisting areas where guardrails are used and guardrails are removed to facilitate the hoisting operation and an employee must lean the access opening or out over the edge of the access opening, is that employee protected from fall hazards by a PFAS? 1926.501(b)(3)

Are employees on walking/working surfaces protected from falling through holes (including skylights) more than 6 feet above lower levels, by PFAS, covers, or guardrail systems erected around such holes? 1926.501(b)(4)(i)

Are employees on a walking/working surface protected from tripping or stepping into or through holes (including skylights) by covers? 1926.501(b)(4)(ii)

Are employees on a walking/working surface protected from objects falling through holes by covers? 1926.501(b)(4)(iii)

Are employees on the face of formwork or reinforcing steel protected from falling 6 feet or more to lower levels by PFAS, safety nets, or positioning device systems? 1926.501(b)(5)

Are employees on ramps, runways or other walkways protected from falling 6 feet or more to lower levels by guardrail systems? 1926.501(b)(6)

Are employees at the edge of an excavation 6 feet or more in depth protected from falling by guardrail systems, fences, or barricades when the excavations are not readily seen because of plant growth or other visual barriers? 1926.501(b)(7)(i)

Are employees at the edge of a well, pit, shaft, and similar excavation 6 feet or more in depth protected from falling by guardrail systems, fences, barricades, or covers? 1926.501(b)(7)(ii)

Is each employee engaged in roofing activities on low-slope roofs, with unprotected sides and edges 6 feet or more above lower levels, protected from falling by guardrail systems, safety net systems, personal fall arrest systems, or a combination of warning line system and guardrail system, warning line system and safety net system, or warning line system and personal fall arrest system, or warning line system and safety monitoring system? 1926.501(b)(10)

Is each employee on a steep roof with unprotected sides and edges 6 feet or more above lower levels protected from falling by guardrail systems with toeboards, safety net systems, or personal fall arrest systems? 1926.501(b)(11)

When an employee is exposed to falling objects, does the employer have each employee wear a hard hat and implement one of the following measures: erect toeboards, screens, or guardrail systems to prevent objects from falling from higher levels; or, erect a canopy structure and keep potential fall objects far enough from the edge of the higher level so that those objects would not go over the edge if they were accidentally displaced; or, barricade the area to which objects could fall, prohibit employees from entering the barricaded area, and keep objects that may fall far enough away from the edge of a higher level so that those objects would not go over the edge if they were accidentally displaced? 1926.501(c)

§1926.502—Fall protection systems criteria and practices.

Is the top edge height of top rails, or equivalent guardrail system members, 42 inches plus or minus 3 inches above the walking/working level? 1926.502(b)(1)

Are midrails, screens, mesh, intermediate vertical members, or equivalent intermediate structural members installed between the top edge of the guardrail system and the walking/working surface when there is no wall or parapet wall at least 21 inches high? 1926.502(b)(2)

Are guardrail systems capable of withstanding, without failure, a force of at least 200 pounds applied within 2 inches of the top edge, in any outward or downward direction, at any point along the top edge? 1926.502(b)(3)

When the 200 pound (890 N) test load specified in paragraph (b)(3) of this section is applied in a downward direction, does the top edge of the guardrail deflect to a height at least 39 inches above the walking/working level? 1926.502(b)(4)

Are top rails and midrails at least ¼ inch nominal diameter or thickness and flagged at not more than 6-foot intervals with high-visibility material? 1926.502(b)(9)

When guardrail systems are used at hoisting areas, is a chain, gate or removable guardrail section placed across the access opening between guardrail sections when hoisting operations are not taking place? 1926.502 (b)(10)

When guardrail systems are used around holes which are used as points of access (such as ladderways), are they provided with a gate, or be so offset that a person cannot walk directly into the hole? 1926.502 (b)(13)

Are safety nets installed no more than 30 feet below the walking working surface? 1926.502(c)(1)

Is the potential fall area from the walking/working surface on bridges to the net unobstructed? 1926.502(c)(1)

Are safety nets extended outward from the outermost projection of the work surface 8 to 13 feet depending on the potential fall distance? 1926.502(c)(2)

When the employer can demonstrate that it is unreasonable to perform a drop-test, does the employer (or a designated competent person) certify that the net and net installation is in compliance with the provisions of this section by preparing a certification record prior to the net being used as a fall protection system? 1926.452(c)(4)(ii)

Are dee-rings and snaphooks proof-tested to a minimum tensile load of 3,600 pounds (16 kN) without cracking, breaking, or taking permanent deformation? 1926.502(d)(4)

Are lifelines protected against being cut or abraded? 1926.502(d)(11)

Are anchorages used for attachment of PFAS independent of any anchorage being used to support or suspend platforms and capable of supporting at least 5,000 pounds per employee attached; or are designed, installed, and used as part of a complete PFAS which maintains a safety factor of at least two, and under the supervision of a qualified person? 1926.502(d)(15)

When stopping a fall, does the PFAS limit maximum arresting force on an employee to 1,800 pounds when used with a body harness? 1926.502(d)(16)(ii)

Is the PFAS rigged such that an employee can neither free fall more than 6 feet, nor contact any lower level? 1926.502(d)(16)(iii)

Is the attachment point of the body harness located in the center of the wearer's back near shoulder level, or above the wearer's head? 1926.502(d)(17)

Are PFAS inspected prior to each use for wear, damage and other deterioration, and are defective components removed from service? 1926.502(d)(21)

Are PFAS not attached to guardrail systems, nor are they attached to hoists except as specified in other subparts of this part? 1926.502(d)(23)

Is the warning line erected around all sides of the roof work area? 1926.502(f)(1)

Are points of access, materials handling areas, storage areas, and hoisting areas connected to the work area by an access path formed by two warning lines? 1926.502(f)(1)(iii)

When the path to a point of access is not in use, is a rope, wire, chain, or other barricade, equivalent in strength and height to the warning line, placed across the path at the point where the path intersects the warning line erected around the work area, or is the path offset such that a person cannot walk directly into the work area? 1926.502(f)(1)(iv)

Is the rope, wire, or chain flagged at not more than 6-foot intervals with high-visibility material? 1926.502(f)(2)(i)

Is the rope, wire, or chain rigged and supported in such a way that its lowest point (including sag) is no less than 34 inches from the walking/working surface and its highest point is no more than 39 inches from the walking/working surface? 1926.502(f)(2)(ii)

Are no employees allowed in the area between a roof edge and a warning line unless the employee is performing roofing work in that area? 1926.502(f)(3)

When used to control access to areas where leading edge and other operations are taking place, is the controlled access zone defined by a control line or by any other means that restricts access? 1926.502(g)(1)

When control lines are used, are they erected not less than 6 feet nor more than 25 feet from the unprotected or leading edge, except when erecting precast concrete members? 1926.502(g)(1)(i)

When erecting precast concrete members, is the control line erected not less than 6 feet nor more than 60 feet or half the length of the member being erected, whichever is less, from the leading edge? 1926.502(g)(1)(ii)

Is the safety monitor on the same walking/working surface and within visual sighting distance of the employee being monitored? 1926.502(h)(1)(iii)

Does the safety monitor have no other responsibilities, which could take the monitor's attention from the monitoring function? 1926.502(h)(1)(v)

Are all other covers capable of supporting, without failure, at least twice the weight of employees, equipment, and materials that may be imposed on the cover at any one time? 1926.502(i)(2)

Are hole covers coded and secured over holes? 1926.502(i)(3-4)

Are toeboards, screens or canopies installed to protect employees below from falling objects? 1926.502(j)

§1926.503—Training requirements.

Does the employer provide a training program for each employee who might be exposed to fall hazards? 1926.503(a)(1)

Subpart N–Helicopters, Hoists, Elevators, and Conveyors

§1926.552—Material hoists, personnel hoists, and elevators.

Are people prohibited from riding on material hoist except for the purpose of inspection and maintenance? 1926.552(b)(1)(ii)

Are hoistway entrances protected by substantial gates or bars? 1926.552(b)(2)

Is overhead protective covering provided on the top of every material hoist cage or platform? 1926.552(b)(3)

Are hoistway door or gates on personnel hoists at least 6 feet 6 inches high? 1926.552(c)(4)

Are hoistway doors or gates provided with mechanical locks which cannot be operated from landing side and are accessible only to persons in car? 1926.552(c)(4)

Are all hoists inspected and tested at not more than 3-month intervals and certification records are kept? 1926.552(c)(15)

§1926.554—Overhead hoists.

Is the safe working load for overhead hoists, as determined by the manufacturer, indicated on the hoist, and this safe working load is not being exceeded? 1926.554(a)(1)

§1926.555—Conveyors.

Are conveyor systems equipped with an audible warning signal to be sounded immediately before starting up the conveyor? 1926.555(a)(1)

Where a conveyor passes over work areas, aisles, or thoroughfares, are suitable guards provided to protect employees required to work below the conveyors? 1926.555(a)(5)

Are conveyors locked out and properly tagged while employees perform repair or maintenance work? 1926.555 (a)(7)

Subpart O—Motor Vehicles, Mechanized Equipment, and Marine Operations

§1926.600—Equipment.

Does all equipment left unattended at night, adjacent to a highway in normal use or adjacent to construction site areas where work is in progress, have appropriate lights or reflectors, or barricades equipped with appropriate lights or reflectors, to identify the location of the equipment? 1926.600(a)(1)

Are safety tire racks, cages, or equivalent protective devices provided and used when inflating, mounting or dismounting tires installed on split rims or locking rings? 1926.600(a)(2)

Are bulldozer and scraper blades, end-loader buckets, dump bodies, and similar equipment, either fully lowered or blocked when being repaired or when not in use? 1926.600(a)(3)(i)

Are parking brakes set on whenever the equipment is parked, and are wheels chocked when parked on an incline? 1926.600(a)(3)(ii)

Does all equipment covered by this subpart comply with the proper requirements when working or being moved in the vicinity of power lines or energized transmitters, except where electrical distribution and transmission lines have been deenergized and visibly grounded at point of work or where insulating barriers, not a part of or an attachment to the equipment or machinery, have been erected to prevent physical contact with the lines? 1926.600(a)(6)

§1926.601—Motor vehicles.

Do all vehicles have a service brake system, an emergency brake system, and a parking brake system maintained in operable condition? 1926.601(b)(1)

Are all vehicles equipped with an audible adequate warning device at the operator's station and in an operable condition? 1926.601(b)(3)

Is motor vehicle equipment having an obstructed view to the rear not used unless the vehicle has a reverse signal alarm audible above the surrounding noise level, or the vehicle is backed up only when an observer signals that it is safe to do so? 1926.601(b)(4)

Are all vehicles with cabs equipped with windshields and powered wipers? Are cracked and broken glass replaced? Are vehicles operating in areas or under conditions that cause fogging or frosting of the windshields equipped with operable defogging or defrosting devices? 1926.601(b)(5)

Do vehicles used to transport employees have seats firmly secured and adequate for the number of employees to be carried? 1926.601(b)(8)

Do all motor vehicles have seat belts and anchorages installed? 1926.601(b)(9)

Are trucks with dump bodies (beds) equipped with a positive means of support, permanently attached, and capable of being locked in position to prevent accidental lowering of the body while maintenance or inspection work is being done? 1926.601(b)(10)

Are operating levers controlling hoisting or dumping devices on haulage bodies equipped with a latch or other device which will prevent accidental starting or tripping of the mechanism? 1926.601(b)(11)

Are trip handles for tailgates of dump trucks so arranged that, in dumping, the operator will be in the clear? 1926.601(b)(12)

Are all vehicles in use inspected at the beginning of each shift to assure that all parts, equipment, and accessories affecting safety operations are in safe operating condition and free of damage? 1926.601(b)(14)

§1926.602—Material handling equipment.

Are seat belts provided on all earth-moving equipment except those not equipped with ROPS and those designed for a standup operation? 1926.602(a)(2)

Does the employer not move or cause to be moved construction equipment or vehicles upon any access roadway or grade unless the access roadway or grade is constructed and maintained to accommodate safely the movement of the equipment and vehicles involved? 1926.602(a)(3)(i)

Does all bi-directional earthmoving equipment have a horn in operable condition? 1926.602(a)(9)(i)

Is all earthmoving or compacting equipment with an obstructed rear view equipped with a reverse signal alarm or an employee signals that it is safe to do so? 1926.602(a)(9)(ii)

Do lift trucks, stackers, etc., have the rated capacity clearly posted on the vehicle? 1926.602(c)(1)(i)

Are all high lift rider industrial trucks equipped with overhead guards? 1926.602(c)(1)(v)

Do all industrial trucks in use meet the applicable requirements of design, construction, stability, inspection, testing, maintenance, and operation, as defined in American National Standards Institute B56.1-1969, Safety Standards for Powered Industrial Trucks? 1926.602(c)(vi)

Are unauthorized personnel not permitted to ride on powered industrial trucks? 1926.602(c)(vii)

As an additional precaution for the protection of personnel being elevated, is a safety platform firmly secured to the lifting carriage and/or forks used? 1926.602(c)(viii)(A)

As an additional precaution for the protection of personnel being elevated, are means provided whereby personnel on the platform can shut off power to the truck? 1926.602(c)(viii)(B)

Does the employer ensure that each powered industrial truck operator is competent to operate a powered industrial truck safely, as demonstrated by the successful completion of the training and evaluation specified in this paragraph (l)?1926.602(d)[3]

§1926.603—Pile driving equipment.

Do boilers and piping systems which are a part of, or used with, pile driving equipment meet the applicable requirements of the American Society of Mechanical Engineers, Power Boilers (section I)? 1926.603(a)(1)

Do all pressure vessels which are a part of, or used with, pile driving equipment meet the applicable requirements of the American Society of Mechanical Engineers, Pressure Vessels (section VIII)? 1926.603(a)(2)

Is overhead protection, which will not obscure the vision of the operator and which meets the requirements of subpart N of this part, provided? Is protection the equivalent of 2-inch planking or other solid material of equivalent strength? 1926.603(a)(3)

Are stop blocks provided for the leads to prevent the hammer from being raised against the head block? 1926.603(a)(4)

Is a blocking device, capable of safely supporting the weight of the hammer, provided for placement in the leads under the hammer at all times while employees are working under the hammer? 1926.603(a)(5)

Are guards provided across the top of the head block to prevent the cable from jumping out of the sheaves? 1926.603(a)(6)

When the leads must be inclined in the driving of batter piles, are provisions made to stabilize the leads? 1926.603(a)(7)

Are fixed leads provided with ladder, and adequate rings, or similar attachment points, so that the loft worker may engage his safety belt lanyard to the leads? If the leads are provided with loft platforms(s), are such platform(s) protected by standard guardrails? 1926.603(a)(8)

Is steam hose leading to a steam hammer or jet pipe securely attached to the hammer with an adequate length of at least ¼-inch diameter chain or cable to prevent whipping in the event the joint at the hammer is broken? Are air hammer hoses provided with the same protection as required for steam lines? 1926.603(a)(9)

---

[3] The requirements applicable to construction work under this paragraph are identical to those set forth at §1910.178(l) of this chapter.

Are safety chains, or equivalent means, provided for each hose connection to prevent the line from thrashing around in case the coupling becomes disconnected? 1926.603(a)(10)

Do steam line controls consist of two shutoff valves, one of which is a quick-acting lever type within easy reach of the hammer operator? 1926.603(a)(11)

Are guys, outriggers, thrustouts, or counterbalances being provided as necessary to maintain stability of pile driver rigs? 1926.603(a)(12)

Do engineers and winchmen accept signals only from the designated signalmen? 1926.603(c)(1)

Are all employees kept clear when piling is being hoisted into the leads? 1926.603(c)(2)

When piles are being driven in an excavated pit, are the walls of the pit sloped to the angle of repose, or sheet-piled and braced? 1926.603(c)(3)

When steel tube piles are being "blown out," are employees kept well beyond the range of falling materials? 1926.603(c)(4)

When it is necessary to cut off the tops of driven piles, are pile driving operations suspended except where the cutting operations are located at least twice the length of the longest pile from the driver? 1926.603(c)(5)

When driving jacked piles, are all access pits provided with ladders and bulkheaded curbs to prevent material from falling into the pit? 1926.603(c)(6)

§1926.604—Site clearing.

Is all equipment used in site clearing operations equipped with rollover guards? 1926.604(a)(2)

§1926.605—Marine operations and equipment.

Are ramps for access of vehicles to or between barges of adequate strength, provided with side boards, well maintained, and properly secured? 1926.605(b)(1)

Unless employees can step safely to or from the wharf, float, barge, or river towboat, is either a ramp, meeting the requirements of paragraph (b)(1) of this section, or a safe walkway, provided? 1926.605(b)(2)

Subpart P–Excavations

§1926.651—Specific excavation requirements.

Are all surface encumbrances that are located so as to create a hazard to employees removed or supported, as necessary, to safeguard employees? 1926.651(a)

Has the estimated location of underground utility installations been determined prior to opening an excavation? 1926.651(b)(1)

Are utility companies or owners contacted within established or customary local response times, advised of the proposed work, and asked to establish the location of the utility underground installations prior to the start of actual excavation? 1926.651(b)(2)

In trenches more than 4 feet deep, are stairways, ladders, or ramps located so that lateral travel to them is no more than 25 feet? 1926.651(c)(2)

Are employees exposed to vehicular traffic wearing warning vests marked or made of reflectorized or high-visibility material? 1926.651(d)

Is a warning system such as barricades, hand or mechanical signals, or stop logs used when mobile equipment approaches the edge of the excavation and the operator does not have a clear and direct view of the edge of the excavation? 1926.651(f)

Are testing and controls used to prevent exposure to harmful levels of atmospheric contaminants and to assure acceptable atmospheric conditions? 1926.651(g)(1)

Do employees not work in excavations in which there is accumulated water, or in excavations in which water is accumulating, unless adequate precautions have been taken to protect employees against the hazards posed by water accumulation? 1926.651(h)(1)

If excavation work interrupts the natural drainage of surface water (such as streams), are diversion ditches, dikes, or other suitable means used to prevent surface water from entering the excavation and to provide adequate drainage of the area adjacent to the excavation? Are excavations subject to runoff from heavy rains inspected by a competent person and in compliance with paragraphs (h)(1) and (h)(2) of this section? 1926.651(h)(3)

Where the stability of adjoining buildings, walls, or other structures is endangered by excavation operations, are support systems such as shoring, bracing, or underpinning provided to ensure the stability of such structures for the protection of employees? 1926.651(i)(1)

Are sidewalks, pavements, and appurtenant structure not undermined unless a support system or another method of protection is provided to protect employees from the possible collapse of such structures? 1926.651(i)(3)

Are excavation or other materials kept at least 2 feet from the edge of the excavations, or are sufficient retaining devices used to prevent materials or equipment from falling or rolling into excavations? 1926.651(j)(2)

Is the excavation inspected by a competent person daily, and after every rainstorm and any hazard increasing occurrence? 1926.651(k)(1)

§1926.652—Requirements for protective systems.

Are employees in an excavation 5 feet deep or more, or with the potential for cave in, protected by an adequate protective system? 1926.652(a)(1)

Are the slopes and configurations of sloping and benching systems selected and constructed by the employer or his designee and in accordance with the requirements? 1926.652(b)

Are designs of support systems shield systems, and other protective systems selected and constructed by the employer or his designee and in accordance with the requirements? 1926.652(c)

Does backfilling progress together with the removal of support systems from excavations? 1926.652(e)(1)(vi)

Is excavation of material to a level no greater than 2 feet below the bottom of the members of a support system only permitted if the system is designed to resist the forces calculated for the full depth of the trench, and there are no indications while the trench is open of a possible loss of soil from behind or below the bottom of the support system? 1926.652(e)(2)(i)

Subpart Q—Concrete and Masonry Construction

§1926.701—General requirements.

Is all protruding reinforcing steel, onto or into which employees could fall, guarded to eliminate the hazard of impalement? 1926.701(b)

Are employees not permitted to ride concrete buckets? 1926.701(d)

Are employees permitted to work under concrete buckets while buckets are being elevated or lowered into position? 1926.701(e)(1)

Are employees not permitted to apply a cement, sand, and water mixture through a pneumatic hose unless the employee is wearing protective head and face equipment? 1926.701(f)

§1926.702—Requirements for equipment and tools.

Are concrete mixers guarded properly? 1926.702(b)(2)

Are powered and rotating type concrete troweling machines that are manually guided equipped with a control switch that will automatically shut off the power whenever the hands of the operator are removed from the equipment handles? 1926.702(c)

Do concrete buggy handles not extend beyond the wheels on either side of the buggy? 1926.702(d)

Are compressed air hoses used on concrete pumping system provided with positive fail-safe joint connectors to prevent separation of sections when pressurized? 1926.702(e)(2)

Do concrete buckets equipped with hydraulic or pneumatic gates have positive safety latches or similar safety devices installed to prevent premature or accidental dumping? 1926.702(f)(1)

Are bull float handles, used where they might contact energized electrical conductors, constructed of nonconductive material, or insulated with a nonconductive sheath whose electrical and mechanical characteristics provide the equivalent protection of a handle constructed of nonconductive material? 1926.702(h)

Are masonry saws guarded with a semicircular enclosure over the blade? 1926.702(i)(1)

Are employees are not permitted to perform maintenance or repair activity on equipment (such as compressors, mixers, screens or pumps used for concrete and masonry construction activities) where the inadvertent operation of the equipment could occur and cause injury, unless all potentially hazardous energy sources have been locked out and tagged? 1926.702(j)(1)

§1926.703—Requirements for cast-in-place concrete.

Is formwork designed, fabricated, erected, supported, braced and maintained so that it will be capable of supporting without failure all vertical and lateral loads that may reasonably be anticipated to be applied to the formwork? 1926.703(a)(1)

Are drawings or plans, including all revisions, for the jack layout, formwork (including shoring equipment), working decks, and scaffolds, available at the jobsite? 1926.703(a)(2)

Is all shoring equipment (including equipment used in reshoring operations) inspected prior to erection to determine that the equipment meets the requirements specified in the formwork drawings? 1926.703(b)(1)

Is erected shoring equipment inspected immediately prior to, during and immediately after concrete placement? 1926.703(b)(3)

Are all base plates, shore heads, extension devices, and adjustment screws in firm contact, and secured when necessary, with the foundation and the form? 1926.703(b)(6)

Are jacks and vertical supports positioned in such a manner that the loads do not exceed the rated capacity of the jacks? 1926.703(c)(4)

Are reinforcing steel for walls, piers, columns, and similar vertical structures adequately supported to prevent overturning and to prevent collapse? 1926.703(d)(1)

Are forms and shores (except those used for slabs on grade and slip forms) not removed until the employer determines that the concrete has gained sufficient strength to support its weight and superimposed loads? 1926.703(e)(1)

§1926.704—Requirements for precast concrete.

Are precast concrete wall units, structural framing, and tilt-up wall panels adequately supported to prevent overturning and to prevent collapse until permanent connections are completed? 1926.704(a)

Are lifting inserts, which are embedded or otherwise attached to tilt-up precast concrete members, capable of supporting at least two times the maximum intended load applied or transmitted to them? 1926.704(b)

Are lifting inserts, which are embedded or otherwise attached to precast concrete members other than the tilt-up members, capable of supporting at least four times the maximum intended load applied or transmitted to them? 1926.704(c)

Is lifting hardware capable of supporting at least five times the maximum intended load applied or transmitted to the lifting hardware? 1926.704(d)

Is no employee permitted under precast concrete members being lifted or tilted into position except those employees required for the erection of those members? 1926.704(e)

§1926.705—Requirements for lift-slab construction operations.

Are lift-slab operations designed and planned by a registered professional engineer who has experience in lift-slab construction, and such plans and designs indicate the prescribed method of erection and provisions for ensuring lateral stability of the building/structure during construction? 1926.705(a)

Is jacking equipment capable of supporting at least two and one-half times the load being lifted during jacking operations and the equipment is not overloaded? 1926.705(d)

Are jacking operations synchronized in such a manner to ensure even and uniform lifting of the slab? 1926.705(g)

When making temporary connections to support slabs, are wedges secured by tack welding, or an equivalent method of securing the wedges to prevent them from falling out of position? Are lifting rods not released until the wedges at that column have been secured? 1926.705(l)

Is the maximum number of manually controlled jacks/lifting units on one slab limited to a number that will permit the operator to maintain the slab level within specified tolerances, and in no case exceeds 14? 1926.705(j)

Are employees who are not essential to the jacking operation not permitted immediately beneath a slab while it is being lifted? 1926.705(k)(2)

§1926.706—Requirements for masonry construction.

Is a limited access zone established whenever a masonry wall is being constructed? 1926.706(a)

Is the limited access zone restricted to entry by employees actively engaged in constructing the wall? 1926.706(a)(4)

Are all masonry walls over 8 feet in height braced or supported to prevent collapse? 1926.706(b)

Subpart R-Steel Erection

§1926.752—Site layout, site-specific erection plan and construction sequence.

Has the controlling contractor ensured that the steel erector is provided in writing that the concrete has cured properly before steel erection begins and any repairs, replacements and modifications were conducted within accordance to 1926.755(b)? 1926.752(a)

Does the steel erection contractor not erect steel unless it has received written notification that the concrete in the footings, piers and walls or the mortar in the masonry piers and walls has attained, on the basis of an appropriate ASTM standard test method of field-cured samples, either 75 percent of the intended minimum compressive design strength or sufficient strength to support the loads imposed during steel erection? 1926.752(b)

Does the controlling contractor ensure that adequate access roads into and through the construction site are provided and maintained? 1926.752(c)(1)

Does the controlling contractor ensure that a firm, properly graded, drained area, readily accessible to the work with adequate space for the safe storage of materials and the safe operation of the erector's equipment, is provided and maintained? 1926.752(c)(2)

Where employers elect, due to conditions specific to the site, to develop alternate means and methods that provide employee protection in accordance with §1926.753(c)(5), §1926.757(a)(4) or §1926.757(e)(4), is a site-specific erection plan developed by a qualified person and available at the work site? 1926.752(e)

§1926.753—Hoisting and rigging.

Are cranes being used in steel erection activities visually inspected prior to each shift by a competent person? 1926.753(c)(1)

Does a qualified rigger inspect the rigging prior to each shift? 1926.753(c)(2)

Is the headache ball, hook or load not being used to transport personnel? 1926.753(c)(3)

Are routes for suspended loads preplanned to ensure that no employee is required to work directly below a suspended load with the exception of employees necessary for the hooking or unhooking of the load? 1926.753(d)(1)

Are a maximum of five members hoisted per lift? 1926.753(e)(1)(ii)

Is the multiple lift rigging assembly rigged with members attached at their center of gravity and maintained reasonably level? 1926.753(e)(4)(i)

Is the multiple lift rigging assembly rigged with members at least 7 feet apart? 1926.753(e)(4)(iii)

§1926.754—Structural steel assembly.

Are permanent floors installed as the erection of structural members progresses, and there are not more than eight stories between the erection floor and the uppermost permanent floor, except where the structural integrity is maintained as a result of the design? 1926.754 (b)(1)

Are fully planked or decked floors or nets maintained within two stories or 30 feet, whichever is less, directly under any erection work being performed? 1926.754 (b)(3)

At the end of the shift or when environmental or jobsite conditions require, is metal decking secured against displacement? 1926.754(e)(1)(v)

Are roof and floor holes and openings decked over? 1926.754(e)(2)(ii)

Are metal decking holes and openings not being cut until immediately prior to being permanently filled? 1926.754(e)(2)(iii)

Are roof and floor opening covers designed to withstand at least twice the weight of employees, equipment, and materials that may be imposed upon it? 1926.754(e)(3)(i)

Are all covers secured to prevent displacement? 1926.754(e)(3)(ii)

Are all covers marked with the word "HOLE" or "COVER"? 1926.754(e)(3)(iii)

Is metal decking laid tightly and immediately secured upon placement to prevent accidental movement or displacement, except as provided in §1926.760(c)? 1926.754(e)(5)(i)

§1926.755—Column anchorage.

Are all columns anchored by a minimum of four anchor bolts? 1926.755(a)(1)

§1926.756—Beams and columns.

During the final placing of solid web structural members, is the load not released from the hoisting line until the members are secured with at least two bolts per connection, of the same size and strength as shown in the erection drawings, drawn up wrench-tight or the equivalent as specified by the project structural engineer of record, except as specified in paragraph (b) of this section? 1926.756(a)(1)

Are solid web structural members used as diagonal bracing secured by at least one bolt per connection drawn up wrench-tight or the equivalent as specified by the project structural engineer of record? 1926.756(b)

§1926.757—Open web steel joists.

Are steel joists and steel joist girders not used as anchorage points for a fall arrest system unless written approval to do so is obtained from a qualified person? 1926.757(a)(9)

§1926.758—Systems-engineered metal buildings.

Are both ends of all steel joists or cold formed joists fully bolted or welded to the support structure before releasing the hoisting cables, allowing an employee on the joist, or allowing any construction loads on the joists? 1926.758(f)

§1926.759—Falling object protection.

Are all materials, equipment and tools, which aren't in use while aloft secured against accidental displacement? 1926.759(a)

Is the controlling contractor barring other construction processes below steel erection unless overhead protection for the employees below is provided? 1926.759(b)

§1926.760—Fall protection.

Is each employee engaged in a steel erection activity who is on a walking/working surface with an unprotected side or edge more than 15 feet above a lower level protected from fall hazards by guardrail systems, safety net systems, personal fall arrest systems, positioning device systems or fall restraint systems? 1926.760 (a)(1)

On multi-story structures, have perimeter safety cables been installed at the final interior and exterior perimeters of floors as soon as the metal decking is installed? 1926.760(a)(2)

Are connectors and employees working in controlled decking zones protected from fall hazards as provided in paragraphs (b) and (c) of this section, respectively? 1926.760(a)(3)

Is each connector protected from fall hazards of more than two stories or 30 feet above a lower level, whichever is less? 1926.760(b)(1)

Has each connector completed connector training in accordance with 1926.761? 1926.760(b)(2)

Is each connector provided with a personnel fall arrest system at heights over 15 and up to 30 feet? 1926.760(b)(3)

Has each employee working in a CDZ completed CDZ training in accordance with §1926.761? 1926.760(c)(4)

Does unsecured decking in a CDZ not exceed 3,000 square feet)? 1926.760(c)(5)

Do perimeter safety cables meet the criteria for guardrail systems in §1926.502? 1926.760(d)(3)

Does fall protection provided by the steel erector remain in the area where steel erection activity has been completed, to be used by other trades, only if the controlling contractor or its authorized representative: has directed the steel erector to leave the fall protection in place; and has inspected and accepted control and responsibility of the fall protection prior to authorizing persons other than steel erectors to work in the area? 1926.760(e)

§1926.761—Training.

Are all employees exposed to fall hazards properly trained? 1926.761(b)

Has special training been provided to employees engaged in multiple lift rigging, connector procedures and CDZ procedures? 1926.761(c)

Subpart S—Underground Construction, Caissons, Cofferdams and Compressed Air

§1926.800—Underground construction.

Is the employer providing access and egress in such a manner that employees are protected from being struck by excavators, haulage machines, trains and other mobile equipment? 1926.800(b)(2)

Is a check-in/check-out system used that will ensure that above-ground personnel can determine an accurate count of the number of persons underground in the event of an emergency? 1926.800(c)

Are all employees instructed in the recognition and avoidance of hazards associated with underground construction activities including, where appropriate, emergency procedures, including evacuation plans and check-in/check-out systems? 1926.800(d)(10)

Is the employer providing self-rescuers approved by the NIOSH? Are the respirators immediately available to all employees at work stations in underground areas where employees might be trapped by smoke or gas? 1926.800(g)(2)

Does the employer store underground no more than a 24-hour supply of diesel fuel for the underground equipment used at the worksite? 1926.800(m)(3)

Is gasoline not carried, stored, or used underground? 1926.800(m)(5)

Are walking and working surfaces of jumbos maintained to prevent the hazards of slipping, tripping and falling? 1926.800(q)(8)(v)(A)

Are all sides of personnel cages enclosed by one-half inch wire mesh (not less than No. 14 gauge or equivalent) to a height of not less than 6 feet? 1926.800(t)(4)(iii)

§1926.801—Caissons.

Are the requirements contained in §1926.803 being complied with in caisson operations where employees are exposed to compressed air working environments? 1926.801(f)

§1926.802—Cofferdams.

At cofferdams, are warning signals for evacuation of employees in case of emergency developed and posted? 1926.802(b)

§1926.803—Compressed air.

Is a competent person present at all times who is designated by and representing the employer, who is familiar with this subpart in all respects, and is responsible for full compliance with this and other applicable subparts? 1926.803(a)(1)

Subpart T—Demolition

§1926.850—Preparatory operations.

Prior to permitting employees to start demolition operations, is an engineering survey made, by a competent person, of the structure to determine the condition of the framing, floors, and walls, and possibility of unplanned collapse of any portion of the structure? 1926.850(a)

When employees are required to work within a structure to be demolished which has been damaged by fire, flood, explosion, or other cause, are the walls or floor shored or braced? 1926.850(b)

Are all electric, gas, water, steam, sewer, and other service lines shut off, capped, or otherwise controlled, outside the building line before demolition work is started? In each case, is any utility company which is involved notified in advance? 1926.850(c)

Where a hazard exists from fragmentation of glass, are such hazards removed? 1926.850(f)

If employees are exposed to the hazard of falling through wall openings, are the openings protected to a height of approximately 42 inches? 1926.850(g)

If debris is dropped through holes in the floor without chutes, is the area onto which the material is dropped completely enclosed with barricades not less than 42 inches high and not less than 6 feet back from the projected edge of the opening above? 1926.850(h)

Are all floor openings, not used as material drops, covered over with material substantial enough to support the weight of any load which may be imposed? 1926.850(i)

Are employee entrances to multi-story structures being demolished completely protected by sidewalk sheds and/or canopies, providing protection from the face of the building for a minimum of 8 feet? 1926.850(k)

§1926.851—Stairs, passageways, and ladders.

Are all stairs, passageways, ladders, and incidental equipment covered by this section periodically inspected and maintained in a clean safe condition? 1926.851(b)

In a multistory building, when a stairwell is being used, is it properly illuminated by either natural or artificial means, and completely and substantially covered over at a point not less than two floors below the floor on which work is being performed; and is access to the floor where the work is in progress through a properly lit, protected, and separate passageway? 1926.851(b)

§1926.852—Chutes.

No material is being dropped to any point lying outside the exterior walls of the structure unless the area is effectively protected? 1926.852(a)

Are all materials chutes, or sections thereof, at an angle of more than 45° from the horizontal, entirely enclosed, except for openings equipped with closures at or about floor level for the insertion of materials? 1926.852(b)

Do chute openings not exceed 48 inches in height measured along the wall of the chute? 1926.852(b)

Is a substantial gate installed in each chute at or near the discharge end? Is a competent employee assigned to control the operation of the gate, and the backing and loading of trucks? 1926.852(c)

When operations are not in progress, is the area surrounding the discharge end of a chute securely closed off? 1926.852(d)

Is any chute opening, into which workmen dump debris, protected by a substantial guardrail approximately 42 inches above the floor or other surface on which the men stand to dump the material? 1926.852(e)

Where the material is dumped from mechanical equipment or wheelbarrows, is a securely attached toeboard or bumper, not less than 4 inches thick and 6 inches high, provided at each chute opening? 1926.852(f)

§1926.856—Removal of walls, floors, and material with equipment.

Do floor openings have curbs or stop-logs to prevent equipment from running over the edge? 1926.856(b)

§1926.858—Removal of steel construction.

When floor arches have been removed, is planking in accordance with §1926.855(b) provided for the workers engaged in razing the steel framing? 1926.858(a)

§1926.859—Mechanical demolition.

During demolition, are continuing inspections by a competent person made as the work progresses to detect hazards resulting from weakened or deteriorated floors, or walls, or loosened material? 1926.859(g)

Subpart U–Blasting and the Use of Explosives

§1926.900—General provisions.

Does the employer permit only authorized and qualified persons to handle and use explosives? 1926.900(a)

Are smoking, firearms, matches, open flame lamps and other fires, flame or heat producing devices, and sparks prohibited in or near explosive magazines and while explosives are being handled, transported, or used? 1926.900(b)

Are all explosives accounted for at all times? 1926.900(d)

Are explosives not in use kept in a locked magazine? 1926.900(d)

Are due precautions taken to prevent accidental discharge of electric blasting caps from current induced by radar, radio transmitters, lighting, adjacent powerlines, dust storms and other sources of extraneous electricity? 1926.900(k)

§1926.902—Surface transportation of explosives.

Is every vehicle or conveyance used for transporting explosives marked or placarded on both sides, the front, and the rear with the word "EXPLOSIVES" in red letters not less than 4 inches high on white background? 1926.902(h)

Is every motor vehicle transporting explosives left attended? 1926.902(k)

§1926.904—Storage of explosives and blasting agents.

Are explosives and related materials stored in approved facilities? 1926.904(a)

Are blasting caps, electric blasting caps, detonating primers, and primed cartridges stored in magazines separate from other explosives or blasting agent? 1926.904(b)

§1926.905—Loading of explosives or blasting agents.

Is tamping done only with wood rods or plastic tamping poles without exposed metal parts, but nonsparking metal connectors may be used for jointed poles? 1926.905(c)

§1926.907—Use of safety fuse.

Is the so-called "drop fuse" method of dropping or pushing a primer or any explosive with a lighted fuse attached forbidden? 1926.907(k)

§1926.909—Firing the blast.

Is a loud warning signal given by the blaster in charge before that blast is fired? 1926.909(b)

Subpart V-Electric Power Transmission and Distribution

§1926.951—Medical services and first aid.

In addition to the requirements of §1926.50, when employees are performing work on, or associated with, exposed lines or equipment energized at 50 volts or more, are persons with first-aid training available? 1926.951(b)

§1926.963—Testing and test facilities.

Wherever ungrounded terminals of test equipment or apparatus under test may be present, are they treated as energized until tests demonstrate that they are deenergized? 1926.963(d)(1)(ii)

Does the employer ensure either that visible grounds are applied automatically, or that employees using properly insulated tools manually apply visible grounds, to the high-voltage circuits after they are deenergized and before any employee performs work on the circuit or on the item or apparatus under test? 1926.963(d)(2)

§1926.964—Overhead lines and live-line barehand work.

Does the employer ensure that, before employees elevate the boom of an aerial lift, the employees ground the body of the truck or barricade the body of the truck and treat it as energized? 1926.964(c)(11)

§1926.965—Underground electrical installations.

When employees perform work on buried cable or on cable in a manhole or vault, does the employer maintain metallic-sheath continuity, or the cable sheath is treated as energized? 1926.965(i)

Subpart W-Rollover Protective Structures; Overhead Protection

§1926.1000—Scope.

Are all rubber-tired, self-propelled scrapers, rubber-tired front-end loaders, rubber-tired dozers, wheel-type agricultural and industrial tractors, crawler tractors, crawler-type loaders, and motor graders, with or without attachments, that are used in construction work, equipped with rollover protective structures? 1926.1000(a)

Do ROPS meet minimum performance criteria detailed in these standards? 1926.1001-1002

Subpart X—Stairways and Ladders

§1926.1051—General requirements.

Is a ladder or stairway provided at all personnel points of access where there is a break in elevation of 19 inches or more? 1926.1051(a)

Is there always at least one clear point of access to permit free passage of employees between levels of a building or structure? 1926.1051(a)(3-4)

§1926.1052—Stairways.

Are metal pan landings and metal pan treads, when used, secured in place before filling with concrete or other material? 1926.1052(a)(5)

Is each stairway having four or more risers or rising more than 30 inches equipped with: at least one handrail; and one stairrail system along each unprotected side or edge? 1926.1052(c)(1)

Are unprotected sides and edges of stairway landings provided with guardrail systems? 1926.1052(c)(12)

§1926.1053—Ladders.

Are ladder rungs, cleats, and steps parallel, level, and uniformly spaced when the ladder is position for use? 1926.1053(a)(2)

Is a metal spreader or locking device provided on each stepladder to hold the front and back sections in an open position when the ladder is being used? 1926.1053(a)(8)

Do ladder safety devices, and related support systems, for fixed ladders permit the employee using the device to ascend or descend without continually having to hold, push or pull any part of the device, leaving both hands free for climbing? 1926.1053(a)(22)(ii)

When portable ladders are used for access to an upper landing surface, do the ladder side rails extend at least 3 feet above the upper landing surface to which the ladder is used to gain access? 1926.1053(b)(1)

Are ladders used only for the purpose for which they were designed? 1926.1053(b)(4)

Are non-self-supporting ladders used at an angle such that the horizontal distance from the top support to the foot of the ladder is approximately one-quarter of the working length of the ladder? 1926.1053(b)(5)(i)

Are ladders used only on stable and level surfaces unless secured to prevent accidental displacement? 1926.1053(b)(6)

Are ladders placed in any location where they can be displaced by workplace activities or traffic, such as in passageways, doorways, or driveways, secured to prevent accidental displacement, or barricaded to keep the activities or traffic away from the ladder? 1926.1053(b)(8)

Is the area around the top and bottom of ladders kept clear? 1926.1053(b)(9)

Do ladders have nonconductive siderails if they are used where the employee or the ladder could contact exposed energized electrical equipment, except as provided in §1926.955(b) and (c) of this part? 1926.1053(b)(12)

Is the top or top step of a stepladder not used as a step? 1926.1053(b)(13)

Are ladders inspected by a competent person for visible defects on a periodic basis and after any occurrence that could affect their safe use? 1926.1053(b)(15)

Are portable ladders with structural defects either immediately marked in a manner that readily identifies them as defective, or tagged with "Do Not Use" or similar language, and withdrawn from service until repaired? 1926.1053(b)(16)

§1926.1060—Training requirements.

Have all employees been trained to recognize hazards related to ladders and stairways? 1926.1060(a)

Subpart Y–Diving

§1926.1076—Qualifications of dive team.[4]

Does each dive-team member have the experience or training necessary to perform assigned tasks in a safe and healthful manner? 1910.410(a)(1)

Does each dive-team member have experience or training in: the use of tools, equipment and systems relevant to assigned tasks; techniques of the assigned diving mode; and diving operations and emergency procedures? 1910.410(a)(2)

Are all dive-team members trained in cardiopulmonary resuscitation and first aid? 1910.410(a)(3)

Are dive-team members who are exposed to or control the exposure of others to hyperbaric conditions trained in diving-related physics and physiology? 1910.410(a)(4)

Is each dive-team member assigned tasks in accordance with the employee's experience or training, except that limited additional tasks may be assigned to an employee undergoing training provided that these tasks are performed under the direct supervision of an experienced dive-team member? 1910.410(b)(1)

Does the employer not require a dive-team member to be exposed to hyperbaric conditions against the employee's will, except when necessary to complete decompression or treatment procedures? 1910.410(b)(2)

Does the employer not permit a dive-team member to dive or be otherwise exposed to hyperbaric conditions for the duration of any temporary physical impairment or condition which is known to the employer and is likely to affect adversely the safety or health of a dive-team member? 1910.410(b)(3)

Is the employer or an employee designated by the employer at the dive location in charge of all aspects of the diving operation affecting the safety and health of dive-team members? 1910.410(c)(1)

Does the designated person-in-charge have experience and training in the conduct of the assigned diving operation? 1910.410(c)(2)

§1926.1080—Safe practices manual.[5]

Does the employer develop and maintain a safe practices manual which is made available at the dive location to each dive-team member? 1910.420(a)

Does the safe practices manual contain a copy of this standard and the employer's policies for implementing the requirements of this standard? 1910.420(b)(1)

---

[4] The requirements applicable to construction work under this section are identical to those set forth at §1910.410 of this chapter.

[5] The requirements applicable to construction work under this section are identical to those set forth at §1910.420 of this chapter.

For each diving mode engaged in, does the safe practices manual include: safety procedures and checklists for diving operations; assignments and responsibilities of the dive-team members; equipment procedures and checklists; and emergency procedures for fire, equipment failure, adverse environmental conditions, and medical illness and injury? 1910.420(b)(2)

§1926.1081—Pre-dive procedures.[6]

Does the employer keep at the dive location a list of the telephone or call numbers of: an operational decompression chamber (if not at the dive location); accessible hospitals; available physicians; available means of transportation; and the nearest U.S. Coast Guard Rescue Coordination Center? 1910.421(b)

Are there first aid supplies? 1910.421(c)

Does the planning of a diving operation include an assessment of the safety and health aspects of: diving mode; surface and underwater conditions and hazards; breathing-gas supply (including reserves); thermal protection; diving equipment and systems; dive-team assignments and physical fitness of dive-team members (including any impairments known to the employer); repetitive dive designation or residual inert-gas status of dive-team members; decompression and treatment procedures (including altitude corrections); and emergency procedures? 1910.421(d)

Are diving operations coordinated with other activities in the vicinity which are likely to interfere with the diving operation? 1910.421(e)

Are dive-team members briefed on: the tasks to be undertaken; safety procedures for the diving mode; any unusual hazards or environmental conditions likely to affect the safety of the diving operation; and any modifications to operating procedures necessitated by the specific diving operation? 1910.421(f)(1)

Prior to making individual dive-team member assignments, does the employer inquire into the dive-team member's current state of physical fitness, and indicate to the dive-team member the procedure for reporting physical problems or adverse physiological effects during and after the dive? 1910.421(f)(2)

Is the breathing-gas supply system including reserve breathing-gas supplies, masks, helmets, thermal protection, and bell handling mechanism (when appropriate) inspected prior to each dive? 1910.421(g)

When diving from surfaces other than vessels in areas capable of supporting marine traffic, is a rigid replica of the international code flag "A" at least one meter in height displayed at the dive location in a manner which allows all-round visibility, and illuminated during night diving operations? 1910.421(h)

---

[6] The requirements applicable to construction work under this section are identical to those set forth at §1910.421 of this chapter.

§1926.1082—Procedures during dive.[7]

Are means capable of supporting the diver provided for entering and exiting the water? 910.422(b)(1)

Does the means provided for exiting the water extend below the water surface? 1910.422(b)(2)

Are means provided to assist an injured diver from the water or into a bell? 1910.422(b)(3)

Is an operational two-way voice communication system used between: each surface-supplied air or mixed-gas diver and a dive-team member at the dive location or bell (when provided or required); and the bell and the dive location? 1910.422(c)(1)

Is an operational, two-way communication system available at the dive location to obtain emergency assistance? 1910.422(c)(2)

Are decompression, repetitive, and no-decompression tables (as appropriate) at the dive location? 1910.422(d)

Is a depth-time profile, including when appropriate any breathing-gas changes, maintained for each diver during the dive including decompression? 1910.422(e)

Are hand-held electrical tools and equipment de-energized before being placed into or retrieved from the water? 1910.422(f)(1)

Are hand-held power tools not supplied with power from the dive location until requested by the diver? 1910.422(f)(2)

Is a current supply switch to interrupt the current flow to the welding or burning electrode: tended by a dive-team member in voice communication with the diver performing the welding or burning; and kept in the open position except when the diver is welding or burning? 1910.422(g)(1)

Is the welding machine frame grounded? 1910.422(g)(2)

Are welding and burning cables, electrode holders, and connections capable of carrying the maximum current required by the work, and properly insulated? 1910.422(g)(3)

Are insulated gloves provided to divers performing welding and burning operations? 1910.422(g)(4)

Prior to welding or burning on closed compartments, are structures or pipes, which contain a flammable vapor or in which a flammable vapor may be generated by the work, vented, flooded, or purged with a mixture of gases which will not support combustion? 1910.422(g)(5)

---

[7] The requirements applicable to construction work under this section are identical to those set forth at §1910.422 of this chapter.

Do employers transport, store, and use explosives in accordance with this section and the applicable provisions of 29 CFR 1910.109 and 29 CFR 1926.912? 1910.422(h)(1)

Is electrical continuity of explosive circuits not tested until the diver is out of the water? 1910.422(h)(2)

Are explosives not be detonated while the diver is in the water? 1910.422(h(3)

Is the working interval of a dive terminated when: a diver requests termination; a diver fails to respond correctly to communications or signals from a dive-team member; communications are lost and cannot be quickly re-established between the diver and a dive-team member at the dive location, and between the designated person-in-charge and the person controlling the vessel in liveboating operations; or a diver begins to use diver-carried reserve breathing gas or the dive-location reserve breathing gas? 1910.422(i)

§1926.1083—Post-dive procedures.[8]

After the completion of any dive, does the employer: check the physical condition of the diver; instruct the diver to report any physical problems or adverse physiological effects including symptoms of decompression sickness; advise the diver of the location of a decompression chamber which is ready for use; and alert the diver to the potential hazards of flying after diving? 1910.423(b)(1)

For any dive outside the no-decompression limits, deeper than 100 fsw or using mixed-gas as a breathing mixture, does the employer instruct the diver to remain awake and in the vicinity of the decompression chamber which is at the dive location for at least one hour after the dive (including decompression or treatment as appropriate)? 1910.423(b)(2)

Is a decompression chamber capable of recompressing the diver at the surface to a minimum of 165 fsw (6 ATA) available at the dive location for: surface-supplied air diving to depths deeper than 100 fsw and shallower than 220 fsw; mixed-gas diving shallower than 300 fsw; or diving outside the no-decompression limits shallower than 300 fsw? 1910.423(c)(1)

Is a decompression chamber capable of recompressing the diver at the surface to the maximum depth of the dive available at the dive location for dives deeper than 300 fsw? 1910.423(c)(2)

Is the decompression chamber: dual-lock; multi-place; and located within 5 minutes of the dive location? 1910.423(c)(3)

Is the decompression chamber equipped with: a pressure gauge for each pressurized compartment designed for human occupancy; a built-in-breathing-system with a minimum of one mask per occupant; a two-way voice communication system between occupants and a dive-team member at the dive

---

[8] The requirements applicable to construction work under this section are identical to those set forth at §1910.423 of this chapter.

location; a viewport; and illumination capability to light the interior? 1910.423(c)(4)

Are treatment tables, treatment gas appropriate to the diving mode, and sufficient gas to conduct treatment available at the dive location? 1910.423(c)(5)

Is a dive-team member available at the dive location during and for at least one hour after the dive to operate the decompression chamber (when required or provided)? 1910.423(c)(6)

Is the following information recorded and maintained for each diving operation: names of dive-team members including the designated person-in-charge; date, time, and location; diving modes used; general nature of work performed; approximate underwater and surface conditions (visibility, water temperature and current); and maximum depth and bottom time for each diver? 1910.423(d)(1)

For each dive outside the no-decompression limits, deeper than 100 fsw or using mixed-gas, is the following additional information recorded and maintained: depth-time and breathing-gas profiles; decompression table designation (including modification); and elapsed time since last pressure exposure if less than 24 hours or repetitive dive designation for each diver? 1910.423(d)(2)

For each dive in which decompression sickness is suspected or symptoms are evident, is the following additional information recorded and maintained: description of decompression sickness symptoms (including depth and time of onset); and description and results of treatment? 1910.423(d)(3)

Does the employer: investigate and evaluate each incident of decompression sickness based on the recorded information, consideration of the past performance of the decompression table used, and individual susceptibility; take appropriate corrective action to reduce the probability of recurrence of decompression sickness; and prepare a written evaluation of the decompression procedure assessment, including any corrective action taken, within 45 days of the incident of decompression sickness? 1910.423(e)(3)

§1926.1084—SCUBA diving.[9]

Is SCUBA diving not conducted: at depths deeper than 130 fsw; at depths deeper than 100 fsw or outside the no-decompression limits unless a decompression chamber is ready for use; against currents exceeding one (1) knot unless line-tended; or in enclosed or physically confining spaces unless line-tended? 1910.424(b)

Is a standby diver available while a diver is in the water? 1910.424(c)(1)

Is a diver line-tended from the surface, or accompanied by another diver in the water in continuous visual contact during the diving operation? 1910.424(c)(2)

---

[9] The requirements applicable to construction work under this section are identical to those set forth at §1910.424 of this chapter.

Is a diver stationed at the underwater point of entry when diving is conducted in enclosed or physically confining spaces? 1910.424(c)(3)

Is a diver-carried reserve breathing-gas supply provided for each diver consisting of: a manual reserve (J-valve); or an independent reserve cylinder with a separate regulator or connected to the underwater breathing apparatus? 1910.424(c)(4)

Is the valve of the reserve breathing-gas supply in the closed position prior to the dive? 1910.424(c)(5)

§1926.1085—Surface-supplied air diving.[10]

Is surface-supplied air diving not conducted at depths deeper than 190 fsw, except that dives with bottom times of 30 minutes or less may be conducted to depths of 220 fsw? 1910.425(b)81)

Is a decompression chamber ready for use at the dive location for any dive outside the no-decompression limits or deeper than 100 fsw? 1910.425(b)(2)

Is a bell used for dives with an inwater decompression time greater than 120 minutes, except when heavy gear is worn or diving is conducted in physically confining spaces? 1910.425(b)(3)

Is each diver continuously tended while in the water? 1910.425(c)(1)

Is a diver stationed at the underwater point of entry when diving is conducted in enclosed or physically confining spaces? 1910.425(c)(2)

Does each diving operation have a primary breathing-gas supply sufficient to support divers for the duration of the planned dive including decompression? 1910.425(c)(3)

For dives deeper than 100 fsw or outside the no-decompression limits: does a separate dive-team member tend each diver in the water? is a standby diver available while a diver is in the water? is a diver-carried reserve breathing-gas supply provided for each diver except when heavy gear is worn? and is a dive-location reserve breathing-gas supply provided? 1910.425(c)(4)

For heavy gear diving deeper than 100 fsw or outside the no-decompression limits: is an extra breathing-gas hose capable of supplying breathing gas to the diver in the water available to the standby diver? Is an inwater stage provided to divers in the water? 1910.425(c)(5)

Except when heavy gear is worn or where physical space does not permit, is a diver-carried reserve breathing-gas supply provided whenever the diver is prevented by the configuration of the dive area from ascending directly to the surface? 1910.425(c)(6)

---

[10] The requirements applicable to construction work under this section are identical to those set forth at §1910.425 of this chapter.

§1926.1086—Mixed-gas diving.[11]

Is mixed-gas diving conducted only when: a decompression chamber is ready for use at the dive location; and a bell is used at depths greater than 220 fsw or when the dive involves inwater decompression time of greater than 120 minutes, except when heavy gear is worn or when diving in physically confining spaces; or a closed bell is used at depths greater than 300 fsw, except when diving is conducted in physically confining spaces? 1910.426(b)(1)

Does a separate dive-team member tend each diver in the water? 1910.426(c)(1)

Is a standby diver available while a diver is in the water? 1910.426(c)(2)

Is a diver stationed at the underwater point of entry when diving is conducted in enclosed or physically confining spaces? 1910.426(c)(3)

Does each diving operation have a primary breathing-gas supply sufficient to support divers for the duration of the planned dive including decompression? 1910.426(c)(4)

Does each diving operation have a dive-location reserve breathing-gas supply? 1910.426(c)(5)

When heavy gear is worn: is an extra breathing-gas hose capable of supplying breathing gas to the diver in the water available to the standby diver; and is an inwater stage provided to divers in the water? 1910.426(c)(6)

Is an inwater stage provided for divers without access to a bell for dives deeper than 100 fsw or outside the no-decompression limits? 1910.426(c)(7)

When a closed bell is used, is one dive-team member in the bell available and tend to the diver in the water? 1910.426(c)(8)

Except when heavy gear is worn or where physical space does not permit, is a diver-carried reserve breathing-gas supply provided for each diver: diving deeper than 100 fsw or outside the no-decompression limits; or prevented by the configuration of the dive area from directly ascending to the surface? 1910.426(c)(9)

§1926.1087—Liveboating.[12]

Are diving operations involving liveboating not conducted: with an inwater decompression time of greater than 120 minutes; using surface-supplied air at depths deeper than 190 fsw, except that dives with bottom times of 30 minutes or less may be conducted to depths of 220 fsw; using mixed-gas at depths greater than 220 fsw; in rough seas which significantly impede diver mobility or work function; or in other than daylight hours? 1926.427(b)

---

[11] The requirements applicable to construction work under this section are identical to those set forth at §1910.426 of this chapter.
[12] The requirements applicable to construction work under this section are identical to those set forth at §1910.427 of this chapter.

Is the propeller of the vessel stopped before the diver enters or exits the water? 1910.427(c)(1)

Is a device used which minimizes the possibility of entanglement of the diver's hose in the propeller of the vessel? 1910.427(c)(2)

Is two-way voice communication between the designated person-in-charge and the person controlling the vessel available while the diver is in the water? 1910.427(c)(3)

Is a standby diver available while a diver is in the water? 1910.427(c)(4)

Is a diver-carried reserve breathing-gas supply carried by each diver engaged in liveboating operations? 1910.427(c)(5)

§1926.1090—Equipment.[13]

Is each equipment modification, repair, test, calibration or maintenance service recorded by means of a tagging or logging system, and include the date and nature of work performed, and the name or initials of the person performing the work? 1910.430(a)(2)

Are compressors used to supply air to the diver equipped with a volume tank with a check valve on the inlet side, a pressure gauge, a relief valve, and a drain valve? 1910.430(b)(1)

Are air compressor intakes located away from areas containing exhaust or other contaminants? 1910.430(b)(1)

Does respirable air supplied to a diver not contain: a level of carbon monoxide (CO) greater than 20 ppm; a level of carbon dioxide (CO_2) greater than 1,000 ppm; a level of oil mist greater than 5 milligrams per cubic meter; or a noxious or pronounced odor? 1910.430(b)(1)

Is the output of air compressor systems tested for air purity every 6 months by means of samples taken at the connection to the distribution system, except that non-oil lubricated compressors need not be tested for oil mist? 1910.430(b)(1)

Do breathing-gas supply hoses have a working pressure at least equal to the working pressure of the total breathing-gas system? 1910.430(c)(1)(i)

Do breathing-gas supply hoses have a rated bursting pressure at least equal to 4 times the working pressure? 1910.430(c)(1)(ii)

Are breathing-gas supply hoses tested at least annually to 1.5 times their working pressure? 1910.430(c)(1)(iii)

Do breathing-gas supply hoses have their open ends taped, capped or plugged when not in use? 1910.430(c)(1)(iv)

---

[13] The requirements applicable to construction work under this section are identical to those set forth at §1910.430 of this chapter.

Are breathing-gas supply hose connectors made of corrosion-resistant materials? 1910.430(c)(2)(i)

Do breathing-gas supply hose connectors have a working pressure at least equal to the working pressure of the hose to which they are attached? 1910.430(c)(2)(ii)

Are breathing-gas supply hose connectors resistant to accidental disengagement? 1910.430(c)(2)(iii)

Are umbilicals marked in 10-foot increments to 100 feet beginning at the diver's end, and in 50-foot increments thereafter? 1910.430(c)(3)(i)

Are umbilicals made of kink-resistant materials? 1910.430(c)(3)(ii)

Do umbilicals have a working pressure greater than the pressure equivalent to the maximum depth of the dive (relative to the supply source) plus 100 psi? 1910.430(c)(3)(iii)

Are helmets or masks connected directly to the dry suit or other buoyancy-changing equipment equipped with an exhaust valve? 1910.430(d)(1)

Is a dry suit or other buoyancy-changing equipment not directly connected to the helmet or mask equipped with an exhaust valve? 1910.430(d)(2)

When used for SCUBA diving, does a buoyancy compensator have an inflation source separate from the breathing-gas supply? 1910.430(d)(3)

Is an inflatable flotation device capable of maintaining the diver at the surface in a face-up position, having a manually activated inflation source independent of the breathing supply, an oral inflation device, and an exhaust valve used for SCUBA diving? 1910.430(d)(4)

Are compressed gas cylinders designed, constructed and maintained in accordance with the applicable provisions of 29 CFR 1910.101 and 1910.169 through 1910.171? 1910.430(e)(1)

Are compressed gas cylinders stored in a ventilated area and protected from excessive heat? 1910.430(e)(2)

Are compressed gas cylinders secured from falling? 1910.430(e)(3)

Do compressed gas cylinders have shut-off valves recessed into the cylinder or protected by a cap, except when in use or manifolded, or when used for SCUBA diving? 1910.430(e)(4)

Is each decompression chamber manufactured after the effective date of this standard, built and maintained in accordance with the ASME Code or equivalent? 1910.430(f)(1)

Is each decompression chamber manufactured prior to the effective date of this standard maintained in conformity with the code requirements to which it was built, or equivalent? 1910.430(f)(2)

Is each decompression chamber equipped with: means to maintain the atmosphere below a level of 25 percent oxygen by volume; mufflers on intake and exhaust lines, which are regularly inspected and maintained; suction guards on exhaust line openings; and a means for extinguishing fire, which is maintained to minimize sources of ignition and combustible material? 1910.430(f)(3)

Are gauges indicating diver depth which can be read at the dive location used for all dives except SCUBA? 1910.430(g)(1)

Is each depth gauge dead-weight tested or calibrated against a master reference gauge every 6 months, and when there is a discrepancy greater than two percent (2 percent) of full scale between any two equivalent gauges? 1910.430(g)(1)

Is a cylinder pressure gauge capable of being monitored by the diver during the dive worn by each SCUBA diver? 1910.430(g)(1)

Is a timekeeping device available at each dive location? 1910.430(g)(1)

Do surface-supplied air and mixed-gas masks and helmets have: a non-return valve at the attachment point between helmet or mask and hose which closes readily and positively; and an exhaust valve? 1919.430(h)(1)

Do surface-supplied air masks and helmets have a minimum ventilation rate capability of 4.5 acfm at any depth at which they are operated or the capability of maintaining the diver's inspired carbon dioxide partial pressure below 0.02 ATA when the diver is producing carbon dioxide at the rate of 1.6 standard liters per minute? 1919.430(h)(2)

Is equipment used with oxygen or mixtures containing over forty percent (40%) by volume oxygen designed for oxygen service? 1910.430(i)(1)

Are components (except umbilicals) exposed to oxygen or mixtures containing over forty percent (40%) by volume oxygen cleaned of flammable materials before use? 1910.430(i)(2)

Do oxygen systems over 125 psig and compressed air systems over 500 psig have slow-opening shut-off valves? 1910.430(i)(3)

Except when heavy gear is worn, are divers equipped with a weight belt or assembly capable of quick release? 1910.430(j)(1)

Except when heavy gear is worn or in SCUBA diving, does each diver wear a safety harness with: a positive buckling device; an attachment point for the umbilical to prevent strain on the mask or helmet; and a lifting point to distribute the pull force of the line over the diver's body? 1910.430(j)(2)

§1926.1091—Recordkeeping requirements.[14]

Does the employer record the occurrence of any diving-related injury or illness which requires any dive-team member to be hospitalized for 24 hours or more, specifying the circumstances of the incident and the extent of any injuries or illnesses? 1910.440(a)(2)

Upon the request of the Assistant Secretary of Labor [for OSHA], or the Director, National Institute for Occupational Safety and Health, Department of Health and Human Services or their designees, does the employer make available for inspection and copying any record or document required by this standard? 1910.440(b)(1)

Are records and documents required by this standard provided upon request to employees, designated representatives, and the Assistant Secretary in accordance with 29 CFR 1910.1020 (a)-(e) and (g)-(i)? 1910.440(b)(2)

Are safe practices manuals (29 CFR 1910.420), depth-time profiles (29 CFR 1910.422), decompression procedure assessment evaluations (29 CFR 1910.423), and records of hospitalizations (29 CFR 1910.440) provided in the same manner as employee exposure records or analyses using exposure or medical records? Are equipment inspections and testing records which pertain to employees (29 CFR 1910.430) also provided upon request to employees and their designated representatives? 1910.440(b)(2)(i)

Are records and documents required by this standard retained by the employer for the following period:

- safe practices manual (29 CFR 1910.420) – current document only;
- depth-time profile (29 CFR 1910.422) – until completion of the recording of the dive, or until completion of decompression procedure assessment where there has been an incident of decompression sickness;
- recordings of dives (29 CFR 1910.423) – 1 year, except 5 years where there has been an incident of decompression sickness;
- decompression procedure assessment evaluations (29 CFR 1910.423) – 5 years;
- equipment inspections and testing records (29 CFR 1910.430) – current entry or tag, or until equipment is withdrawn from service;
- records of hospitalizations (29 CFR 1910.440) – 5 years? 1910.440(b)(3)

Does the employer also comply with any additional requirements set forth at 29 CFR 1910.1020(h)? 1910.440(b)(4)

---

[14] The requirements applicable to construction work under this section are identical to those set forth at §1910.440 of this chapter.

Subpart Z—Toxic and Hazardous Substances

§1926.1101—Asbestos.

Does the employer ensure that no employee is exposed to an airborne concentration of asbestos in excess of 0.1 fiber per cubic centimeter of air as an eight (8) hour time-weighted average (TWA), as determined by the method prescribed in appendix A to this section, or by an equivalent method? 1926.1101(c)(1)

Does the employer ensure that no employee is exposed to an airborne concentration of asbestos in excess of 1.0 fiber per cubic centimeter of air (1 f/cc) as averaged over a sampling period of thirty (30) minutes, as determined by the method prescribed in appendix A to this section, or by an equivalent method? 1926.1101(c)(2)

On multi-employer worksites, does the employer performing work requiring the establishment of a regulated area inform other employers on the site of the nature of the employer's work with asbestos and/or PACM, of the existence of and requirements pertaining to regulated areas, and the measures taken to ensure that employees of such other employers are not exposed to asbestos? 1926.1101(d)(1)

Is all Class I, II and III asbestos work conducted within regulated areas? 1926.1101(e)(1)

Is the regulated area demarcated in any manner that minimizes the number of persons within the area and protects persons outside the area from exposure to airborne asbestos? 1926.1101(e)(2)

Does the employer ensure that all asbestos work performed within regulated areas is supervised by a competent person? 1926.1101(e)(6)

Does the employer monitor airborne concentrations of asbestos to which employees may be exposed, and has an exposure assessment/personal air sampling been performed to determine degree of employee exposure? 1926.1101(f)(1)

Does each employer who has a workplace or work operation covered by this standard ensure that a "competent person" conducts an exposure assessment immediately before or at the initiation of the operation to ascertain expected exposures during that operation or workplace? 1926.1101(f)(2)(i)

Does the employer use the prescribed engineering controls and work practices in all operations covered by this section, regardless of the levels of exposure? 1926.1101(g)(1)

For employees who use respirators required by this section, does the employer provide each employee an appropriate respirator that complies with the requirements of this paragraph? 1926.1101(h)(1)

Does the employer implement a respiratory protection program in accordance with §1910.134 (b) through (d) (except (d)(1)(iii)), and (f) through (m), which covers each employee required by this section to use a respirator? 1926.1101(h)(2)

Does the employer provide or require the use of protective clothing (coveralls, head covers) for any employee exposed to airborne concentrations of asbestos? 1926.1101(i)(1)

Is contaminated clothing transported in sealed impermeable bags, or other closed, impermeable containers, and labeled in accordance with paragraph (k) of this section? 1926.1101(i)(3)

Does the competent person examine worksuits worn by employees at least once per workshift for rips or tears that may occur during performance of work? 1926.1101(i)(4)(i)

Are hygiene facilities and practices appropriate to the class of ACM work and size of job (less than or greater than 25 linear or 10 square feet)? 1926.1101(j)

Does the employer ensure that each employee has access to labels on containers of asbestos and safety data sheets, and is trained in accordance with the provisions of HCS and paragraphs (k)(9) and (10) of this section? 1926.1101(k)(1)(ii)

Are warning signs that demarcate the regulated area provided and displayed at each location where a regulated area is required to be established by paragraph (e) of this section? Are signs posted at such a distance from such a location that an employee may read the signs and take necessary protective steps before entering the area marked by the signs? 1926.1101(k)(7)

Does the employer train each employee who is likely to be exposed in excess of a PEL, and each employee who performs Class I through IV asbestos operations, in accordance with the requirements of this section? 1926.1101(k)(9)(i)

Are appropriate housekeeping practices followed, such as the use of HEPA filtered vacuuming equipment to collect ACM dust and placing ACM wastes/debris into impermeable, labeled, and sealed containers? 1926.1101(l)

If required, does the employer institute a medical surveillance program for all employees who for a combined total of 30 or more days per year are engaged in Class I, II and III work or are exposed at or above a permissible exposure limit? 1926.1101(m)

Does the employer keep a recordkeeping program for all asbestos related work? 1926.1101(n)

§1926.1127—Cadmium.

Does the employer assure that no employee is exposed to an airborne concentration of cadmium in excess of five micrograms per cubic meter of air (5 µg/m^3), calculated as an eight-hour TWA? 1926.1127(c)

Prior to the performance of any construction work where employees may be potentially exposed to cadmium, does the employer establish the applicability of this standard by determining whether cadmium is present in the workplace and whether there is the possibility that employee exposures will be at or above the action level? 1926.1127(d)(1)(i)

Have determinations of employee exposure been made from breathing-zone air samples that reflect the monitored employee's regular, daily 8-hour TWA exposure to cadmium? 1926.1127(d)(1)(iii)

Has the employer established a regulated area wherever an employee's exposure to airborne concentrations of cadmium is, or can reasonably be expected to be in excess of the PEL? 1926.1127(e)(1)

Does the employer implement engineering and work practice controls to reduce and maintain employee exposure to cadmium at or below the PEL, except to the extent that the employer can demonstrate that such controls are not feasible? 1926.1127(f)(1)(i)

Where employee exposure to cadmium exceeds the PEL and the employer is required to implement controls to comply with the PEL, prior to the commencement of the job does the employer establish and implement a written compliance program to reduce employee exposure to or below the PEL? 1926.1127(f)(5)(i)

For employees who use respirators required by this section, does the employer provide each employee an appropriate respirator that complies with the requirements of this paragraph? 1926.1127(g)(1)

If an employee is exposed to airborne cadmium above the PEL or where skin or eye irritation is associated with cadmium exposure at any level, does the employer provide at no cost to the employee, and assure that the employee uses, appropriate protective work clothing and equipment that prevents contamination of the employee and the employee's garments? 1926.1127(i)(1)

For employees whose airborne exposure to cadmium is above the PEL, does the employer provide clean change rooms, handwashing facilities, showers, and lunchroom facilities that comply with 29 CFR 1926.51? 1926.1127(j)(1)

Does the employer assure that the lunchroom facilities are readily accessible to employees, that tables for eating are maintained free of cadmium, and that no employee in a lunchroom facility is exposed at any time to cadmium at or above a concentration of 2.5 µg/m^3? 1926.1127(j)(4)(i)

Is compressed air not used to remove cadmium from any surface unless the compressed air is used in conjunction with a ventilation system designed to capture the dust cloud created by the compressed air? 1926.1127(k)(6)

Has the employer instituted a medical surveillance program for all employees who are or may be exposed at or above the action level and all employees who perform the following tasks, operations or jobs: Electrical grounding with cadmium welding; cutting, brazing, burning, grinding or welding on surfaces that were painted with cadmium-containing paints; electrical work using cadmium-coated conduit; use of cadmium containing paints; cutting and welding cadmium-plated steel; brazing or welding with cadmium alloys; fusing of reinforced steel by cadmium welding; maintaining or retrofitting cadmium-coated equipment; and, wrecking and demolition where cadmium is present? 1926.1127(l)(1)(i)(A)

Does the employer ensure that each employee has access to labels on containers of cadmium and safety data sheets, and is trained in accordance with the provisions of HCS and paragraph (m)(4) of this section? 1926.1127(m)(1)

§1926.1153—Respirable crystalline silica.

For each employee engaged in a task identified on Table 1, does the employer fully and properly implement the engineering controls, work practices, and respiratory protection specified for the task on Table 1, unless the employer assesses and limits the exposure of the employee to respirable crystalline silica in accordance with paragraph (d) of this section? 1926.1153(c)(1)

For tasks performed indoors or in enclosed areas, does the employer provide a means of exhaust as needed to minimize the accumulation of visible airborne dust? 1926.1153(c)(2)(i)

For tasks performed using wet methods, is water applied at flow rates sufficient to minimize release of visible dust? 1926.1153(c)(2)(ii)

For measures implemented that include an enclosed cab or booth, is it ensured that the enclosed cab or booth is maintained as free as practicable from settled dust; has door seals, closing mechanisms, gaskets and seals that are in good, working condition; is under positive pressure maintained through continuous delivery of fresh air; and has intake air that is filtered through a filter that is MERV-16 or better? 1926.1153(c)(2)(iii)

Are respirators provided to employees who may be over-exposed to silica dust particles? 1926.1153(c)(3)

Where respiratory protection is required by this section, does the employer provide each employee an appropriate respirator that complies with the requirements of this paragraph and 29 CFR 1910.134? 1926.1153(e)(1)

Does the employer not allow dry sweeping or dry brushing where such activity could contribute to employee exposure to respirable crystalline silica unless wet sweeping, HEPA-filtered vacuuming or other methods that minimize the likelihood of exposure are not feasible? 1926.1153(f)(1)

Does the employer not allow compressed air to be used to clean clothing or surfaces where such activity could contribute to employee exposure to respirable crystalline silica? 1926.1153(f)(2)

Does the employer establish and implement an effective written exposure control plan? 1926.1153(g)(1)

Does the employer review and evaluate the effectiveness of the written exposure control plan at least annually and update it as necessary? 1926.1153(g)(2)

Does the employer designate a competent person to make frequent and regular inspections of job sites, materials, and equipment to implement the written exposure control plan? 1926.1153(g)(4)

Does the employer make medical surveillance available at no cost to the employee, and at a reasonable time and place, for each employee who will be required under this section to use a respirator for 30 or more days per year? 1926.1153(h)(1)(i)

Does the employer make available an initial (baseline) medical examination within 30 days after initial assignment, unless the employee has received a medical examination that meets the requirements of this section within the last three years? 1926.1153(h)(2)

Does the employer make available medical examinations that include the procedures described in paragraph (h)(2) of this section (except paragraph (h)(2)(v)) at least every three years, or more frequently if recommended by the PLHCP? 1926.1153(h)(3)

Does the employer ensure that each employee covered by this section can demonstrate knowledge and understanding of at least the following: the health hazards associated with exposure to respirable crystalline silica; specific tasks in the workplace that could result in exposure to respirable crystalline silica; specific measures the employer has implemented to protect employees from exposure to respirable crystalline silica, including engineering controls, work practices, and respirators to be used; the contents of this section; the identity of the competent person designated by the employer in accordance with paragraph (g)(4) of this section; and the purpose and a description of the medical surveillance program required by paragraph (h) of this section? 1926.1153(i)(2)(i)

Does the employer make and maintain an accurate record of all exposure measurements taken to assess employee exposure to respirable crystalline silica, as prescribed in paragraph (d)(2) of this section? 1926.1153(j)(1)(i)

Subpart AA-Confined Spaces in Construction

§1926.1203—General requirements.

Before it begins work at a worksite, does each employer ensure that a competent person identifies all confined spaces in which one or more of the employees it directs may work, and identifies each space that is a permit space, through consideration and evaluation of the elements of that space, including testing as necessary? 1926.1203 (a)

If the workplace contains one or more permit spaces, does the employer who identifies, or who receives notice of, a permit space: inform exposed employees by posting danger signs or by any other equally effective means, of the existence and location of, and the danger posed by, each permit space; and inform, in a timely manner and in a manner other than posting, its employees' authorized representatives and the controlling contractor of the existence and location of, and the danger posed by, each permit space? 1926.1203 (b)

Can the employer demonstrate that continuous forced air ventilation alone is sufficient to maintain that permit space safe for entry, and that, in the event the ventilation system stops working, entrants can exit the space safely? 1926.1203(e)(1)(ii)

Before an employee enters the space, is the internal atmosphere tested, with a calibrated direct-reading instrument, for oxygen content, for flammable gases and vapors, and for potential toxic air contaminants, in that order? 1926.1203(e)(2)(iii)

Is continuous forced air ventilation used, as follows: an employee does not enter the space until the forced air ventilation has eliminated any hazardous atmosphere; the forced air ventilation is so directed as to ventilate the immediate areas where an employee is or will be present within the space and continues until all employees have left the space; the air supply for the forced air ventilation is from a clean source and does not increase the hazards in the space? 1926.1203(e)(2)(v)

Before entry operations begin, does the host employer provide to the controlling contractor information on: the location of each known permit space; the hazards or potential hazards in each space or the reason it is a permit space; and any precautions that the host employer or any previous controlling contractor or entry employer implemented for the protection of employees in the permit space? 1926.1203(h)(1)

Before entry operations begin, does the controlling contractor: obtain the host employer's information about the permit space hazards and previous entry operations; and provide the following information to each entity entering a permit space and any other entity at the worksite whose activities could foreseeably result in a hazard in the permit space: the information received from the host employer;

any additional information the controlling contractor has about the subjects listed in paragraph (h)(1) of this section; and the precautions that the host employer, controlling contractor, or other entry employers implemented for the protection of employees in the permit spaces? 1926.1203(h)(2)

§1926.1204—Permit-required confined space program.

Does the employer implement the measures necessary to prevent unauthorized entry? 1926.1204(a)

Does the employer identify and evaluate the hazards of permit spaces before employees enter them? 1926.1204(b)

Does the employer develop and implement the means, procedures, and practices necessary for safe permit space entry operations? 1926.1204(c)

Does each entry employer provide, maintain, and ensure employees properly use testing and monitoring equipment operable and calibrated as needed? 1926.1204(d)(1)

Does each entry employer provide, maintain, and ensure employees properly use ventilating equipment needed to obtain acceptable entry conditions? 1926.1204(d)(2)

Does each entry employer provide, maintain, and ensure employees properly use communications equipment necessary for compliance with §§1926.1208(c) and 1926.1209(e), including any necessary electronic communication equipment for attendants assessing entrants' status in multiple spaces? 1926.1204(d)(3)

Does each entry employer provide, maintain, and ensure employees properly use lighting equipment that meets the minimum illumination requirements in §1926.56, that is approved for the ignitable or combustible properties of the specific gas, vapor, dust, or fiber that will be present, and that is sufficient to enable employees to see well enough to work safely and to exit the space quickly in an emergency? 1926.1204(d)(5)

Does each entry employer provide, maintain, and ensure employees properly use equipment, such as ladders, needed for safe ingress and egress by authorized entrants? 1926.1204(d)(7)

Does each entry employer provide, maintain, and ensure employees properly use rescue and emergency equipment needed to comply with paragraph (i) of this section, except to the extent that the equipment is provided by rescue services? 1926.1204(d)(8)

Does each entry employer continuously monitor atmospheric hazards unless it can demonstrate that the equipment for continuously monitoring a hazard is not commercially available or that periodic monitoring is of sufficient frequency to ensure that the atmospheric hazard is being controlled at safe levels? 1926.1204(e)(2)

§1926.1206—Entry permit.

Does the entry permit that documents compliance with this section and authorizes entry to a permit space identify equipment, such as personal protective equipment, testing equipment, communications equipment, alarm systems, and rescue equipment, to be provided for compliance with this standard? 1926.1206(n)

§1926.1207—Training.

Does the employer provide training to each employee whose work is regulated by this standard, at no cost to the employee, and ensure that the employee possesses the understanding, knowledge, and skills necessary for the safe performance of the duties assigned under this standard? 1926.1207(a)

Does the employer maintain training records to show that the training required by paragraphs (a) through (c) of this section has been accomplished? 1926.1207(d)

Subpart CC-Cranes and Derricks in Construction

§1926.1402—Ground conditions.

Is the equipment not assembled or used unless ground conditions are firm, drained, and graded to a sufficient extent so that, in conjunction (if necessary) with the use of supporting materials, the equipment manufacturer's specifications for adequate support and degree of level of the equipment are met? 1926.1402(b)

§1926.1403—Assembly/Disassembly— selection of manufacturer or employer procedures.

When assembling or disassembling equipment (or attachments), does the employer comply with all applicable manufacturer prohibitions and comply with either: manufacturer procedures applicable to assembly and disassembly, or employer procedures for assembly and disassembly? 1926.1403

§1926.1404—Assembly/Disassembly— general requirements (applies to all assembly and disassembly operations).

Is assembly/disassembly being directed by a person who meets the criteria for both a competent person and a qualified person, or by a competent person who is assisted by one or more qualified persons ("A/D director")? 1926.1404(a)(1)

When outriggers or stabilizers are used, are all requirements of this section met? 1926.1404(q)

Are the outriggers or stabilizers either fully extended or, if manufacturer procedures permit, deployed as specified in the load chart? 1926.1404(q)(1)

Does the outrigger and stabilizer blocking meet the requirements in paragraphs (h)(2) and (h)(3) of this section (sufficient to sustain loads and maintain stability)? 1926.1404(q)(5)(i)

Is the outrigger and stabilizer blocking placed only under the outrigger or stabilizer float/pad of the jack or, where the outrigger or stabilizer is designed without a jack, under the outer bearing surface of the extended outrigger or stabilizer beam? 1926.1404(q)(5)(ii)

§1926.1407—Power line safety (up to 350 kV)—assembly and disassembly.

Before assembling or disassembling equipment, does the employer determine if any part of the equipment, load line, or load (including rigging and lifting accessories) could get, in the direction or area of assembly/disassembly, closer than 20 feet to a power line during the assembly/disassembly process? 1926.1407(a)

If any part of the equipment, load line, or load could get closer than 20 feet then does the employer meet one of these requirements:

- confirms from the utility owner/operator that the power line has been deenergized and visibly grounded at the worksite;
- ensures that no part of the equipment, load line or load, gets closer than 20 feet to the power line by implementing the measures specified in paragraph (b) of this section;
- determines the line's voltage and the minimum clearance distance permitted under Table A (see §1926.1408); and follows the requirements in paragraph (b) of this section if it determines any part of the equipment, load line, or load could get closer than the minimum clearance distance to the power line permitted under Table A (see §1926.1408)? 1926.1407(a)

Where necessary, does the dedicated spotter use equipment that enables the dedicated spotter to communicate directly with the operator? 1926.1407(b)(3)(i)(C)

§1926.1408—Power line safety (up to 350 kV)--equipment operations.

Is there an elevated warning line, barricade, or line of signs, in view of the operator? 1926.1408(b)(3)

§1926.1412—Inspections.

Does a competent person begin a visual inspection prior to each shift the equipment will be used, which is completed before or during that shift? 1926.1412(d)(1)

Is the equipment inspected each month it is in service in accordance with paragraph (d) of this section (each shift)? 1926.1412(e)(1)

Does a qualified person make thorough annual inspections on the equipment, and does the employer that conducts the inspection maintain for a minimum of 12 months the records of the dates, results of inspections, and the signature of the inspector? 1926.1412(f)(1, 2 & 7)

§1926.1415—Safety devises.

Does the equipment covered by this subpart have all the required safety devices installed and maintained? 1926.1415(a)

§1926.1416—Operational aids.

Does the equipment covered by this subpart have all the listed operational aids installed and maintained? 1926.1416(a)

Does all equipment covered by this subpart, unless otherwise specified, use a boom angle indicator? 1926.1416(d)(1)(i)(A)

Are telescopic boom cranes manufactured after February 28, 1992, equipped with a device which automatically prevents damage from contact between the load block, overhaul ball, or similar component, and the boom tip (or fixed upper block or similar component)? 1926.1416(d)(3)(i)

§1926.1417—Operation.

Does the employer comply with all manufacturer procedures applicable to the operational functions of equipment, including its use with attachments? 1926.1417(a)

Are the procedures applicable to the operation of the equipment, including rated capacities (load charts), recommended operating speeds, special hazard warnings, instructions, and operator's manual, readily available in the cab at all times for use by the operator? 1926.1417(c)(1)

Does the operator not leave the controls while the load is suspended, except where all exceptions in this section are met? 1926.1417(e)(1)

Is a tag or restraint line used if necessary to prevent rotation of the load that would be hazardous? 1926.1417(w)

§1926.1419—Signals—general requirements.

Are the signals used (hand, voice, audible, or new), and means of transmitting the signals to the operator (such as direct line of sight, video, radio, etc.), appropriate for the site conditions? 1926.1419(e)

§1926.1422—Signals—hand signal chart.

Are hand signal charts either posted on the equipment or conspicuously posted in the vicinity of the hoisting operations? 1926.1422

§1926.1423—Fall protection.

For a PFAS to be anchored to the crane/derrick's hook (or other part of the load line), has a qualified person determined that the set-up and rated capacity of the crane/derrick (including the hook, load line and rigging) meets or exceeds the requirements in §1926.502(d)(15)? 1926.1423(j)

§1926.1424—Work area control.

To prevent employees from entering swing radius hazard areas, does the employer train each employee assigned to work on or near the equipment ("authorized personnel") in how to recognize struck-by and pinch/crush hazard areas posed by the rotating superstructure; and erect and maintain control lines, warning lines, railings or similar barriers to mark the boundaries of the hazard areas? 1926.1424(a)(2)

§1926.1425—Keeping clear of the load.

While the operator is not moving a suspended load, are employees prohibited within the fall zone, except for employees engaged in hooking, unhooking or guiding a load; engaged in the initial attachment of the load to a component or structure; or operating a concrete hopper or concrete bucket? 1926.1425(b)

Are hooks with self-closing latches or their equivalent being used (exception: "J" hooks are permitted to be used for setting wooden trusses)? 1926.1425(c)(2)

Are the materials being rigged by a qualified rigger? 1926.1425(c)(3)

§1926.1427—Operator training, certification, and evaluation.

Does the employer ensure that each operator is trained, certified/licensed, and evaluated in accordance with this section before operating any equipment covered under subpart CC, except for the equipment listed in paragraph (a)(2) of this section? 1926.1427(a)

Is the operator accredited by a nationally recognized accrediting agency based on that agency's determination that industry-recognized criteria for written testing materials, practical examinations, test administration, grading, facilities/equipment, and personnel have been met? 1926.1427(d)(1)(i)

Through an evaluation, does the employer ensure that each operator is properly qualified? 1926.1427(f)(1-7)

§1926.1428—Signal person qualifications.

Does the employer of the signal person ensure that each signal person meets the Qualification Requirements (paragraph (c) of this section) prior to giving any signals? 1926.1428(a)

§1926.1431—Hoisting personnel.

Are cranes or derricks only used to hoist employees on a personnel platform when conventional means are more hazardous or impossible? 1926.1431(a)

When using equipment to hoist employees, are the employees in a personnel platform that meets the requirements of paragraph (e) of this section? 1926.1431(b)(1)

Does the personnel platform meet all design criteria and platform specifications required by this standard? 1926.1431(e)

Are materials and tools secured to prevent displacement? 1926.1431(f)(3)(i)

Are tag lines used when necessary to control the platform? 1926.1431(k)(5)

Is hoisting personnel within 20 feet of a power line that is up to 350 kV, and hoisting personnel within 50 feet of a power line that is over 350 kV, prohibited, except for work covered by subpart V of this part? 1926.1431(n)

§1926.1432—Multiple-crane/derrick lifts—supplemental requirements.

Before beginning a crane/derrick operation in which more than one crane/derrick will be supporting the load, is an operation plan made that meets the following requirements: it is developed by a qualified person; it is designed to ensure that the requirements of this subpart are met; and where the qualified person determines it is necessary, does the employer ensure that engineering expertise is provided? 1926.1432(a)

§1926.1433—Design, construction and testing.

Is an accessible fire extinguisher on the equipment? 1926.1433(d)(6)

§1926.1435—Tower cranes.

Is the weight of the load determined from a source recognized by the industry (such as the load's manufacturer), or by a calculation method recognized by the industry (such as calculating a steel beam from measured dimensions and a known per foot weight), or by other equally reliable means? 1926.1435(d)(5)(v)

Before each crane component is erected, is it inspected by a qualified person for damage or excessive wear? 1926.1435(f)(2)

In addition to the items that must be inspected under §1926.1412(f), are all turntable and tower bolts inspected annually for proper condition and torque? 1926.1435(f)(5)

§1926.1441—Equipment with a rated hoisting/lifting capacity of 2,000 pounds or less.

Does the employer ensure that equipment covered by this section manufactured after November 8, 2011, have either an anti two-block device that meets the requirements of §1926.1416(d)(3), or is designed so that in the event of a two-block situation, no damage or load failure will occur (for example, by using a power unit that stalls in response to a two-block situation)? 1926.1441(d)(2)

OSHA Most Frequently Cited Serious Violations
Construction Industry FY 2020

Most Frequently Cited Serious Violations

Construction Industry FY2020

OSHA Federal Standards
October 1, 2019 – September 30, 2020

Most Frequently Cited Serious Violations in Construction 2020

29 CFR 1926 Subparts | **1926 Overall MFC**

Subpart	Standard	Description	Count
M	.501(b)(13)	Fall Protection – Residential construction	3598
E	.102(a)(1)	Eye & Face Protection – Use of appropriate protection	1354
X	.1053(b)(1)	Ladders – Not extended 3 feet above landing	1311
M	.503(a)(1)	Fall Protection – Training for those exposed to fall hazards	1141
M	.501(b)(1)	Fall Protection – Unprotected sides & edges	879
E	.100(a)	Head Protection – Use of protection	799
L	.453(b)(2)(v)	Aerial Lifts – Fall protection	530
C	.21(b)(2)	General Safety & Health Provision – Inspections by a competent person	487
C	.20(b)(2)	General Safety & Health Provision – Frequent and regular inspections	460
C	.20(b)(1)	General Safety & Health Provision – Employer to maintain program	452

Number of Serious Violations – FY 2020

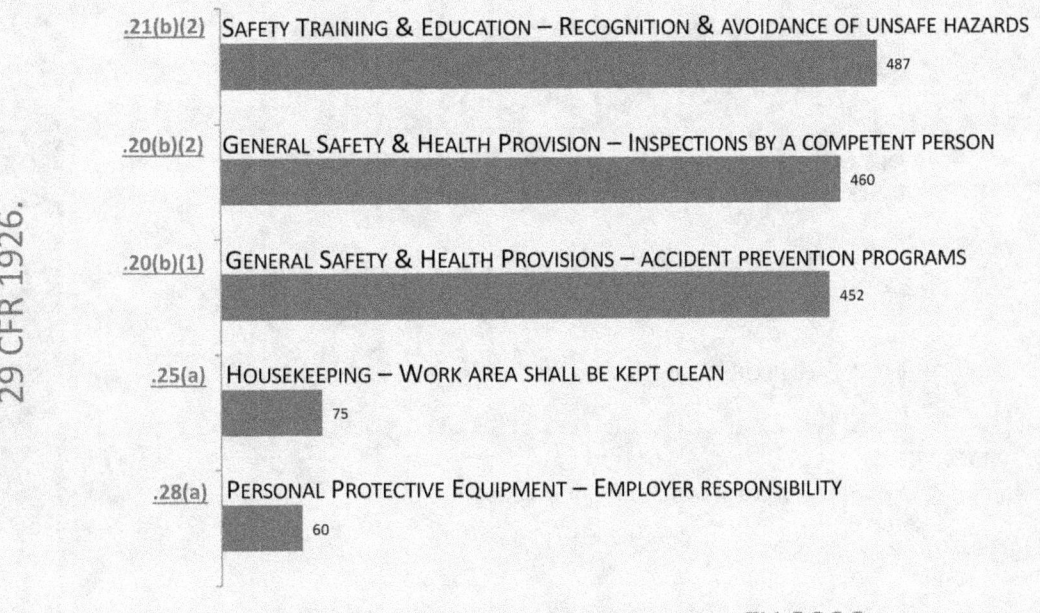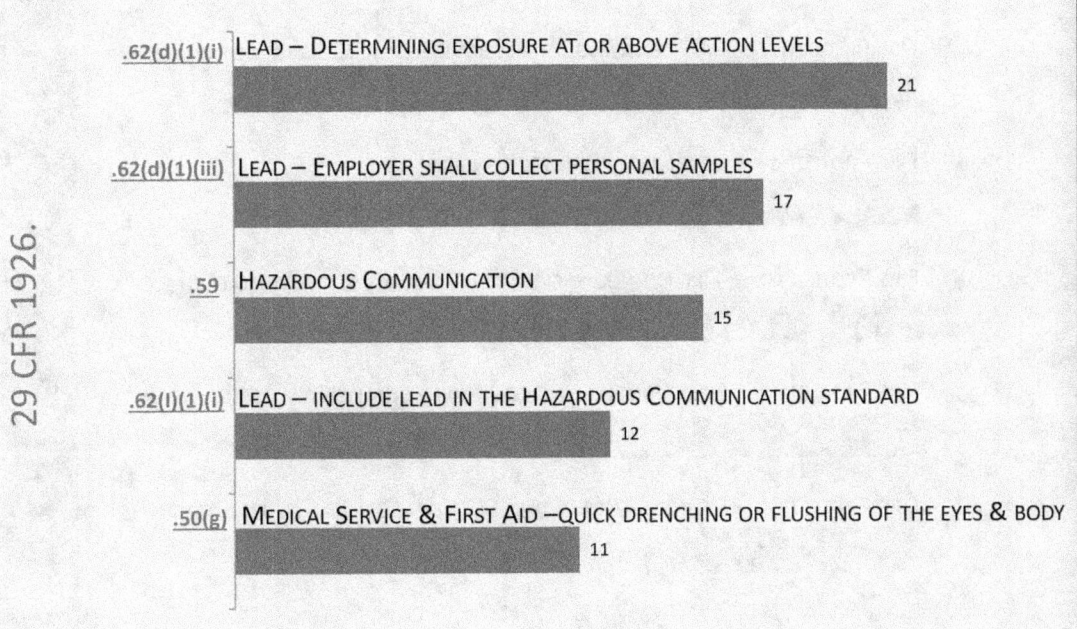

Personal Protective & Life Saving Equipment
[1926.95 – .107]

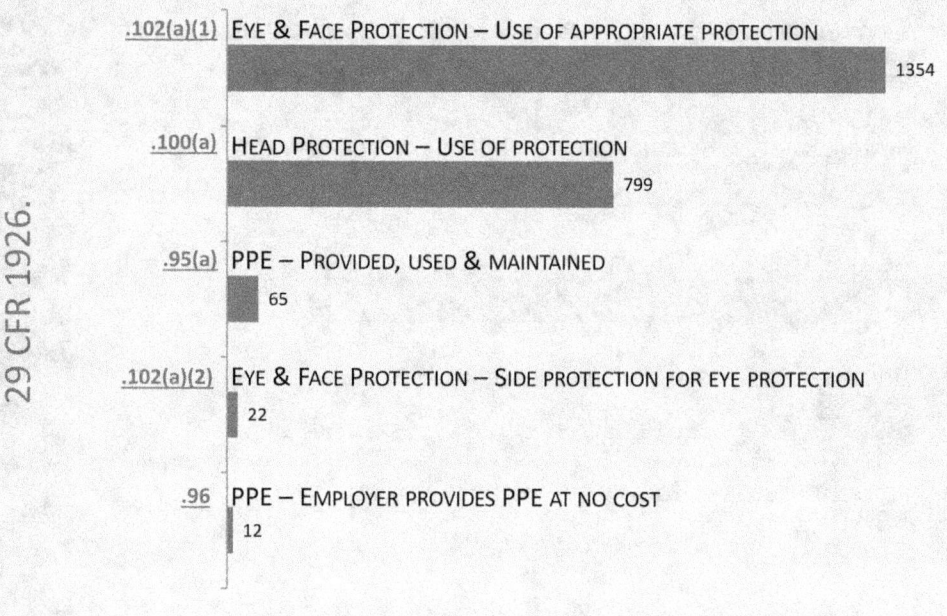

Fire Protection & Prevention
[1926.150 – .159]

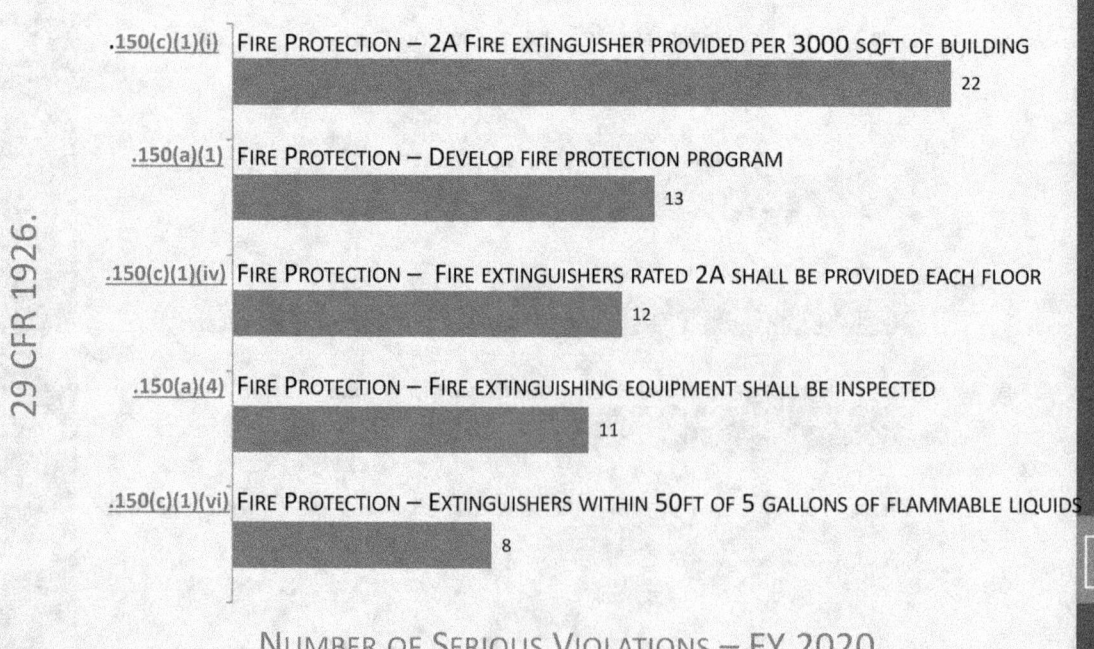

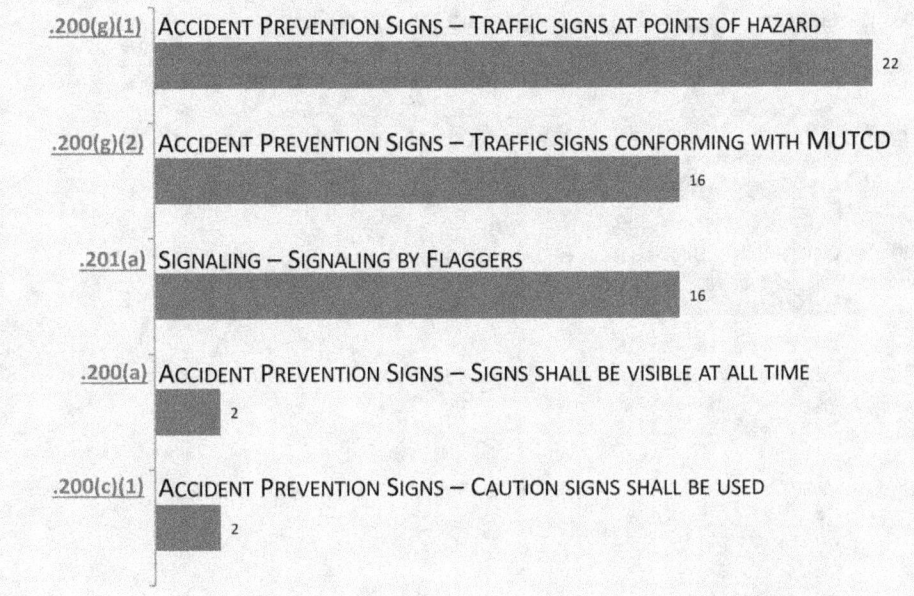

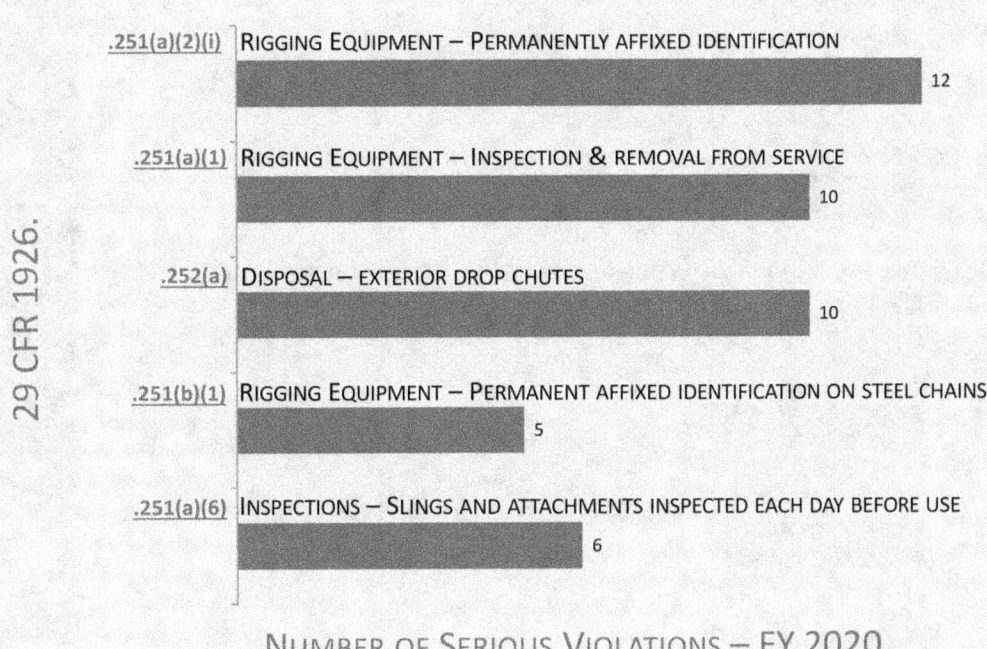

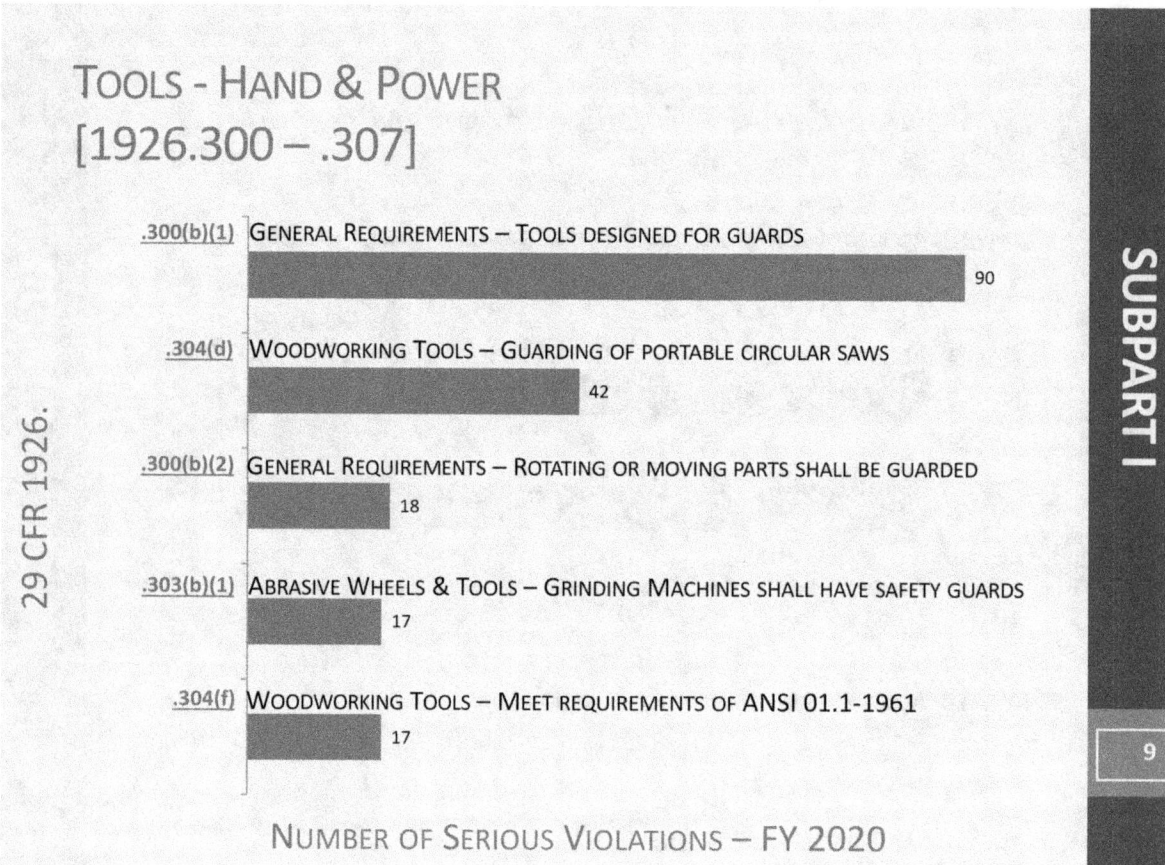

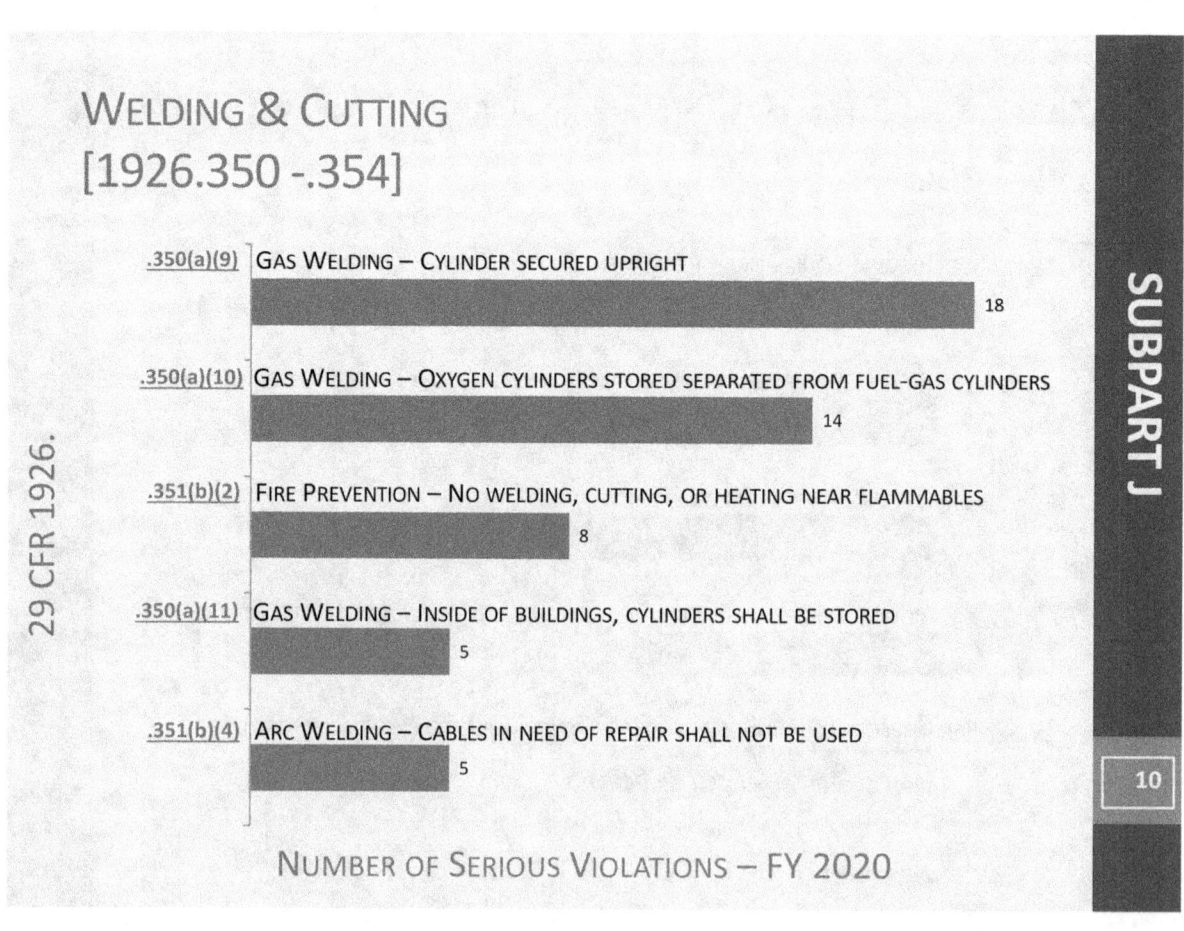

Electrical
[1926.400 – .449]

29 CFR 1926.

- **.416(a)(1)** General Requirements – No work near any part of an electrical circuit: **111**
- **.405(g)(2)(iv)** Wiring Methods – Strain relief: **104**
- **.416(e)(1)** General Requirements – Worn & frayed cords and cables: **102**
- **.404(f)(6)** Wiring Design – Grounding path: **100**
- **.403(b)(2)** General Requirements – Installation & use: **68**

Number of Serious Violations – FY 2020

SUBPART K — 11

Scaffolds
[1926.450 – .454]

29 CFR 1926.

- **.453(b)(2)(v)** Aerial Lifts – Fall protection while in basket: **530**
- **.451(g)(1)** General Requirements – Fall protection above 10 feet: **419**
- **.451(e)(1)** General Requirements – Safe access above 2 feet: **364**
- **.451(b)(1)** General Requirements – All working levels shall be full planked: **296**
- **.454(a)** Training Requirements – Training by a qualified person: **276**

Number of Serious Violations – FY 2020

SUBPART L — 12

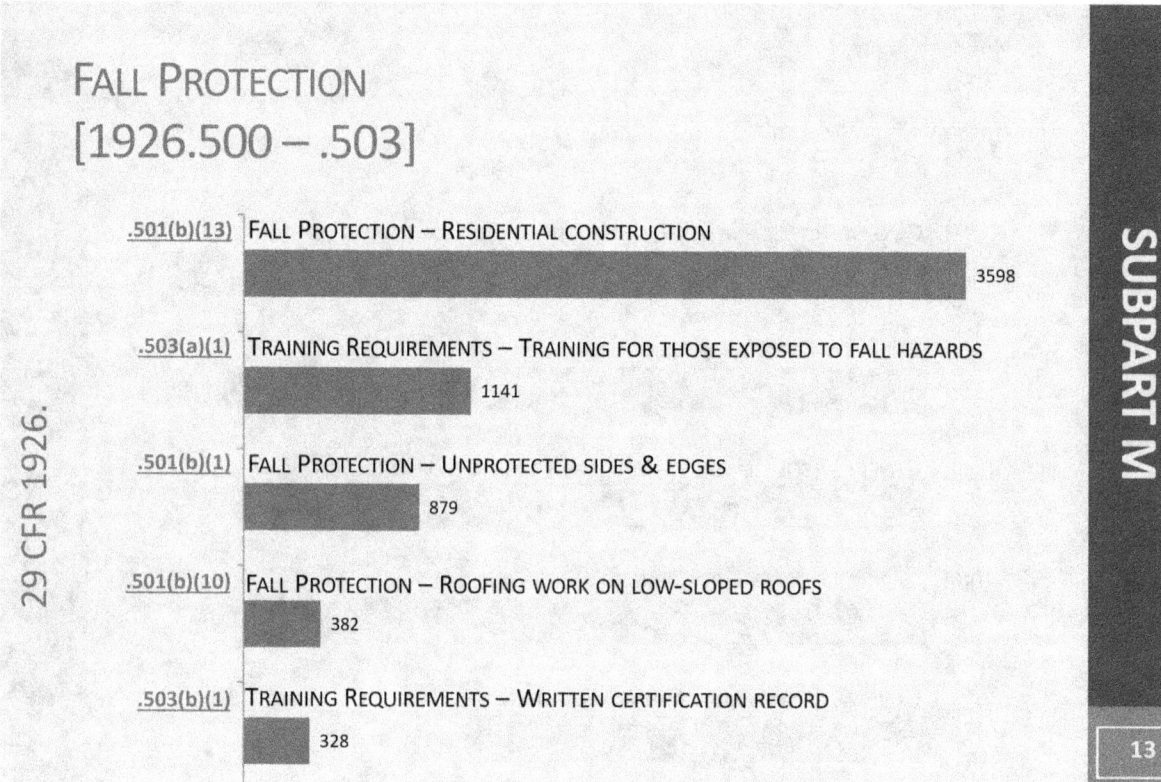
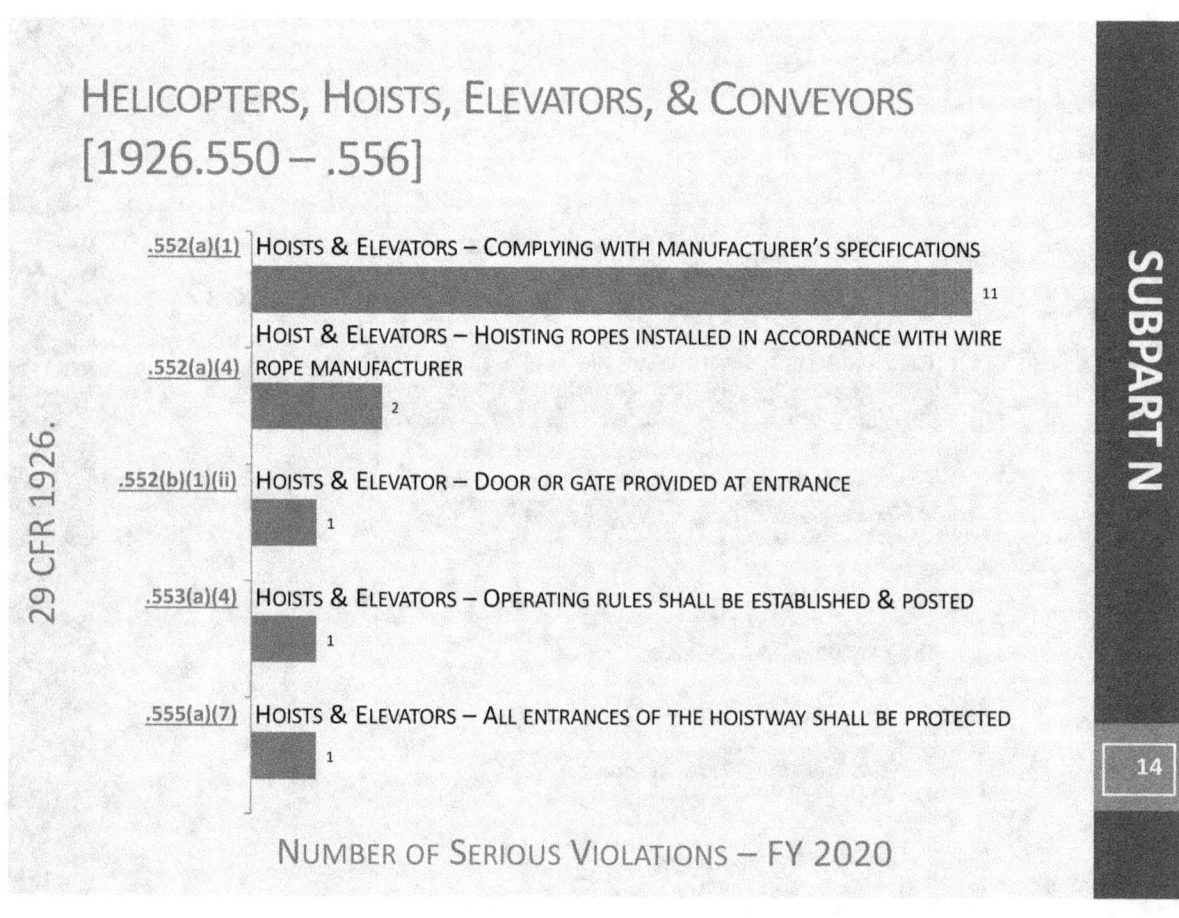

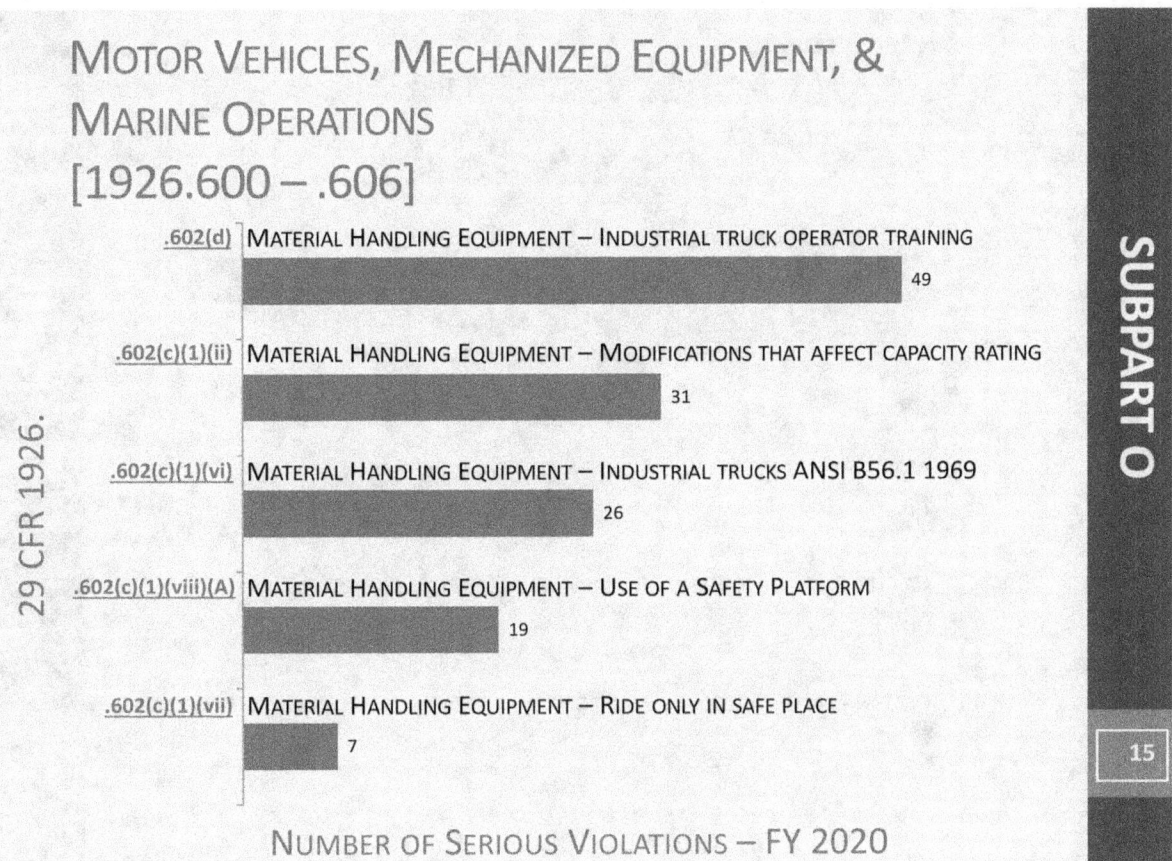

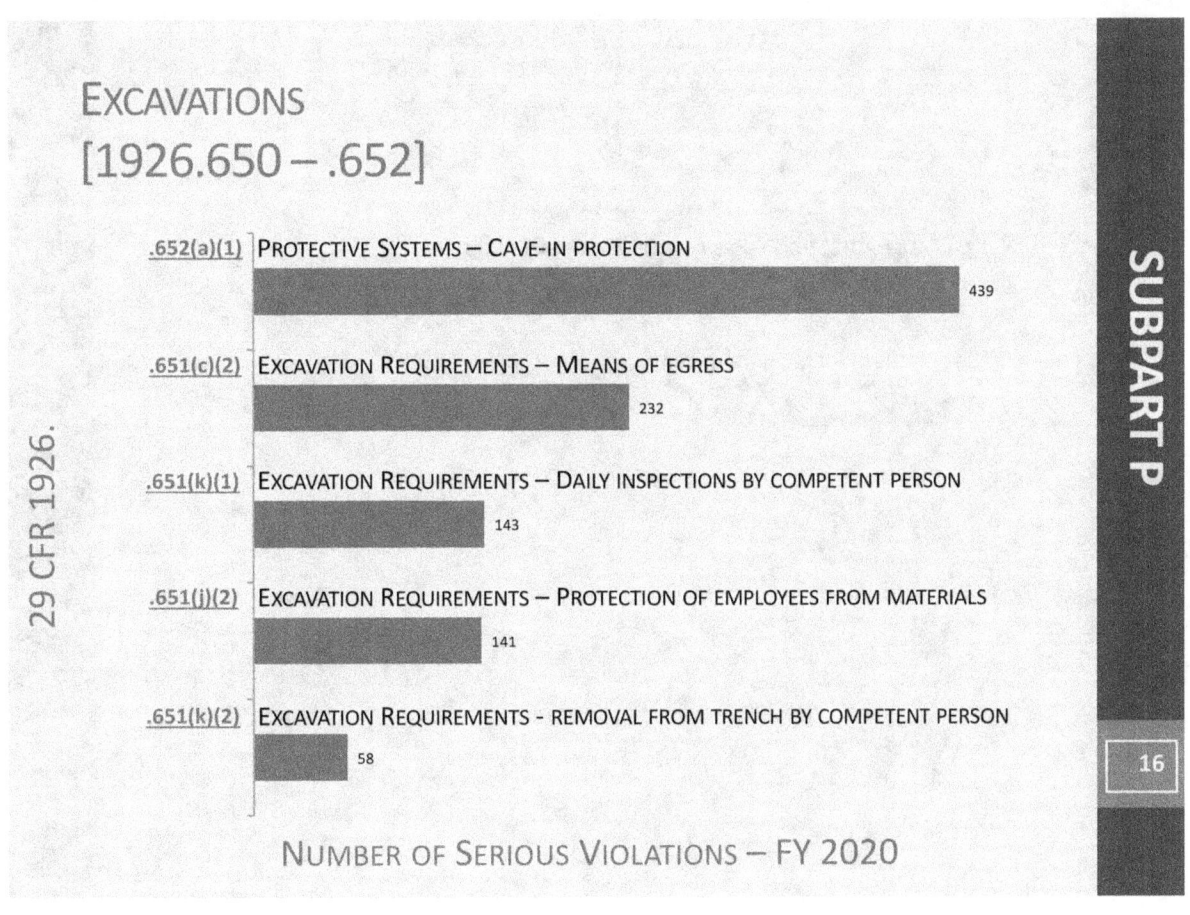

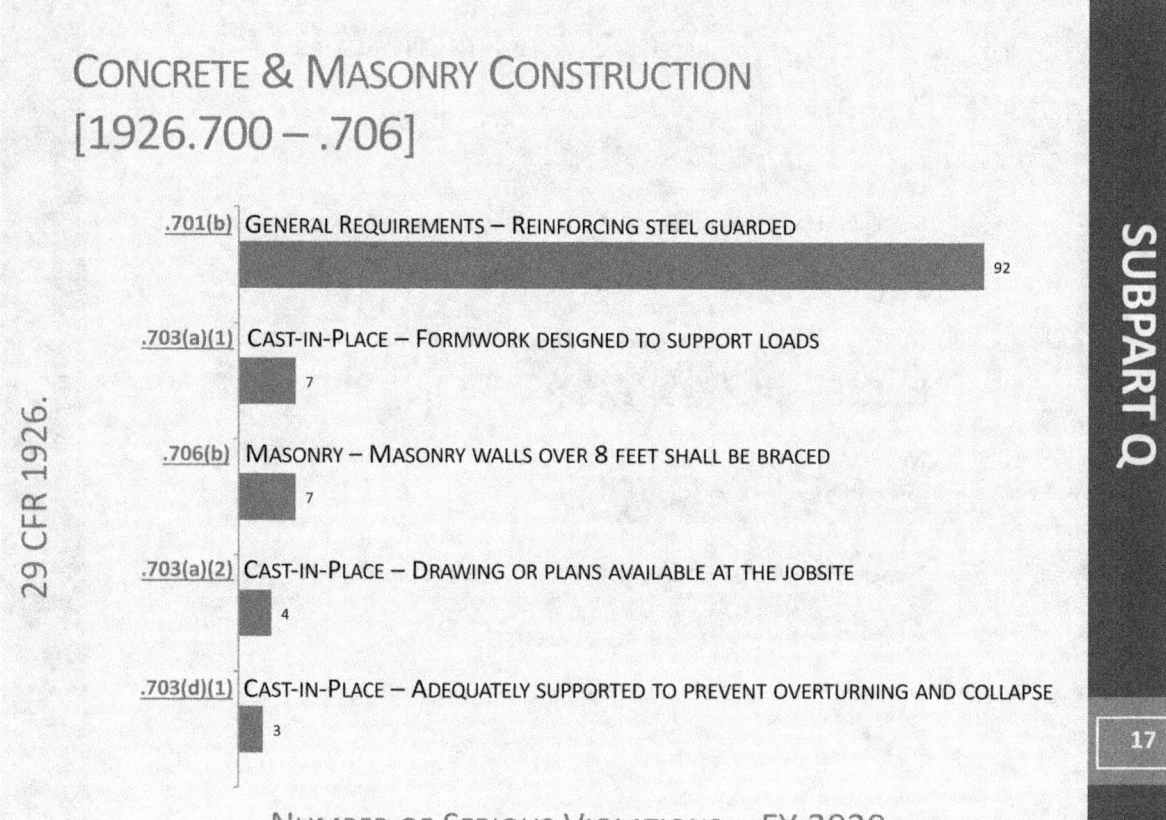
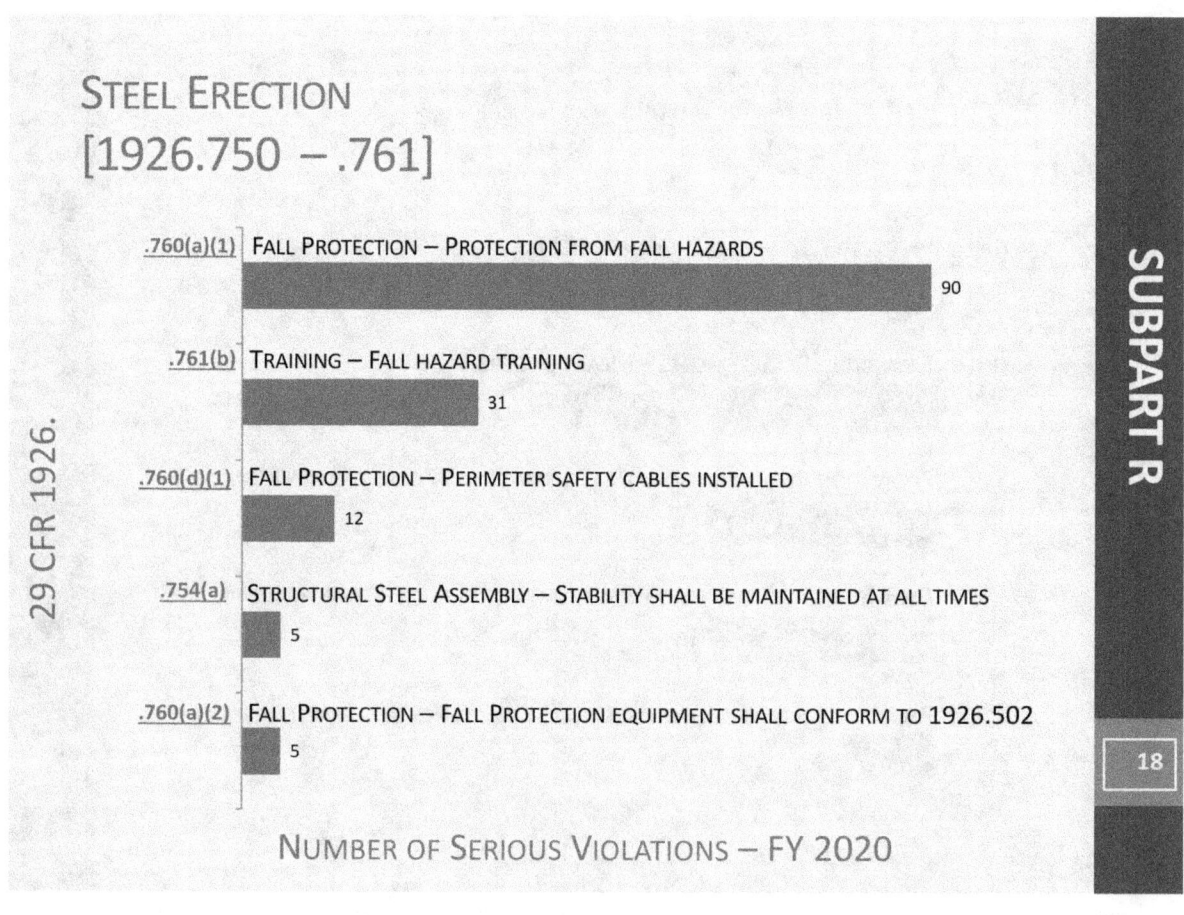

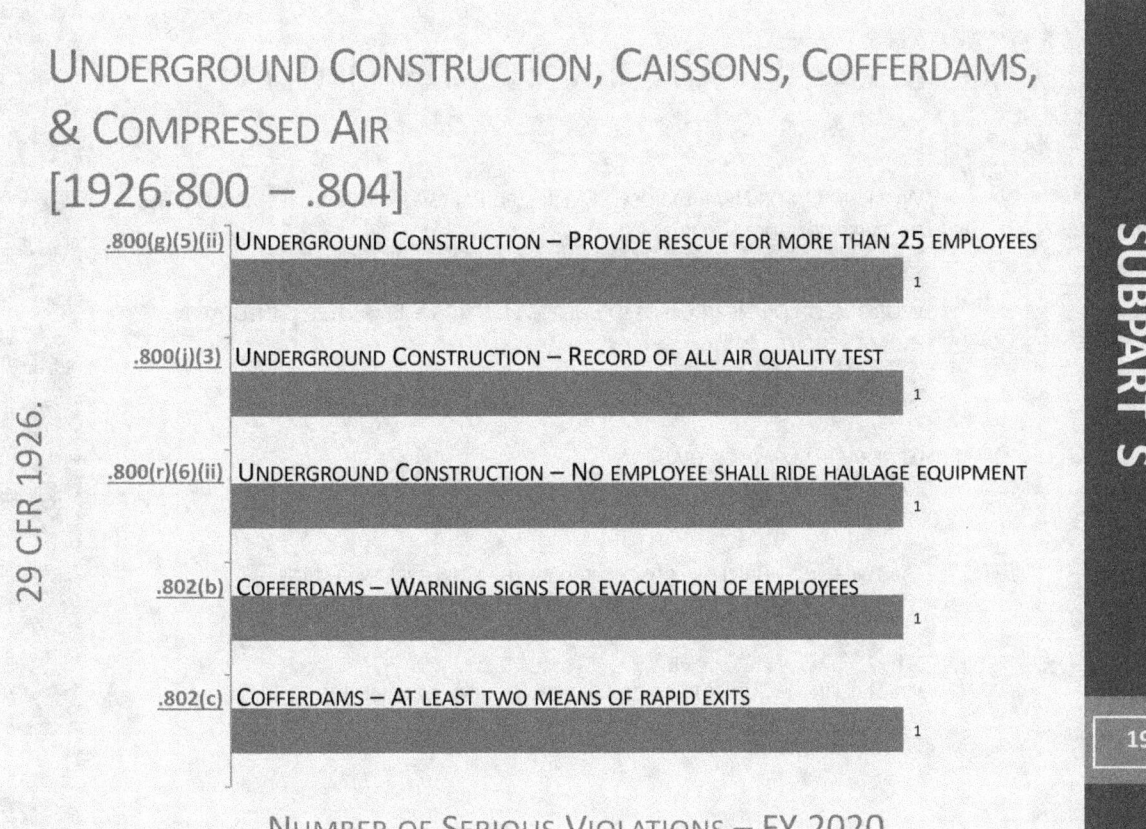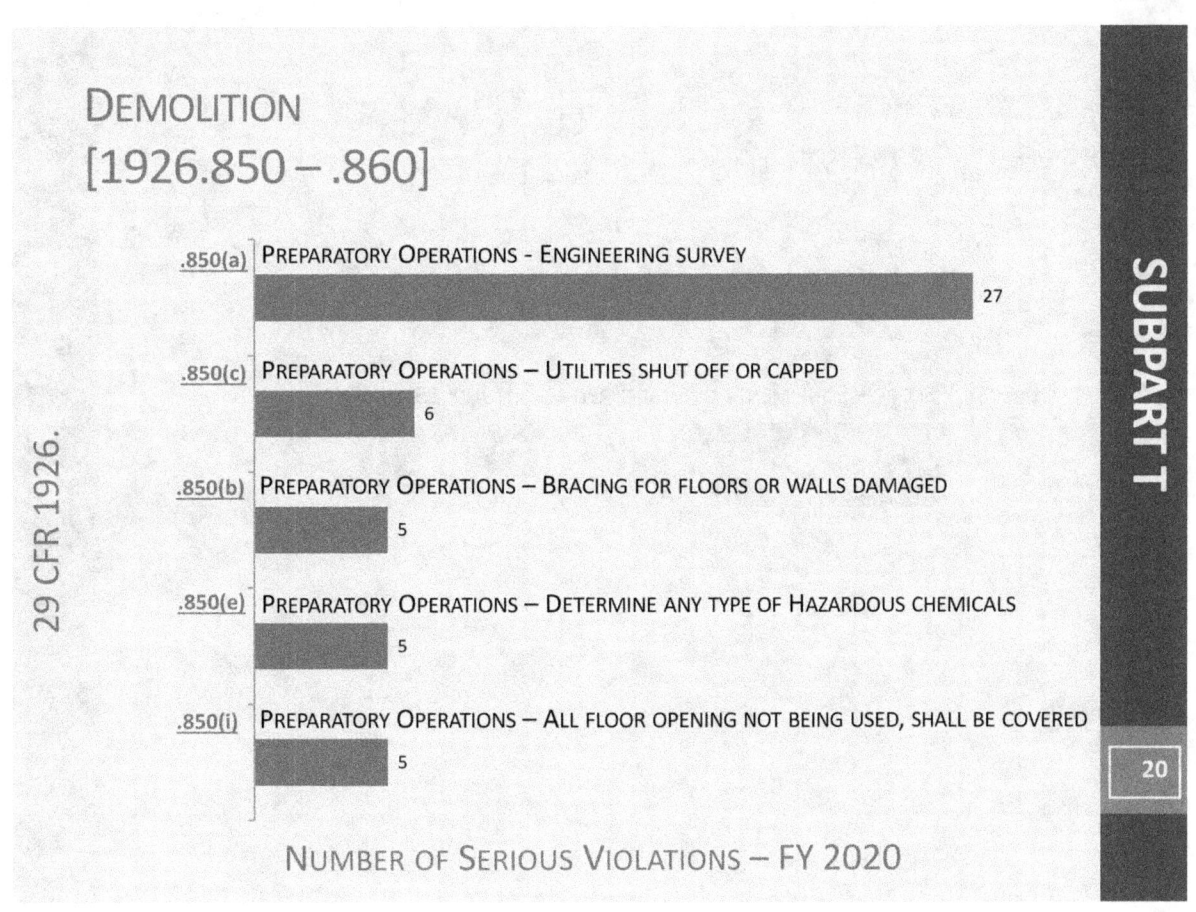

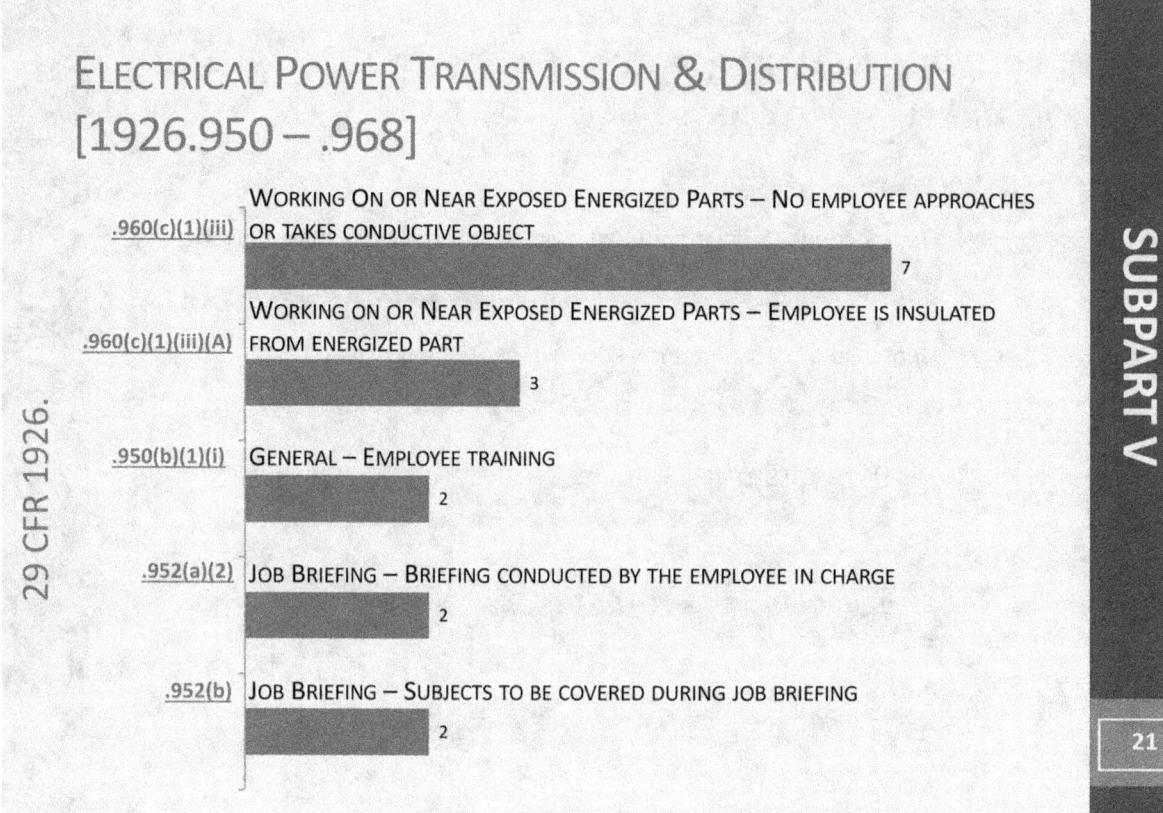

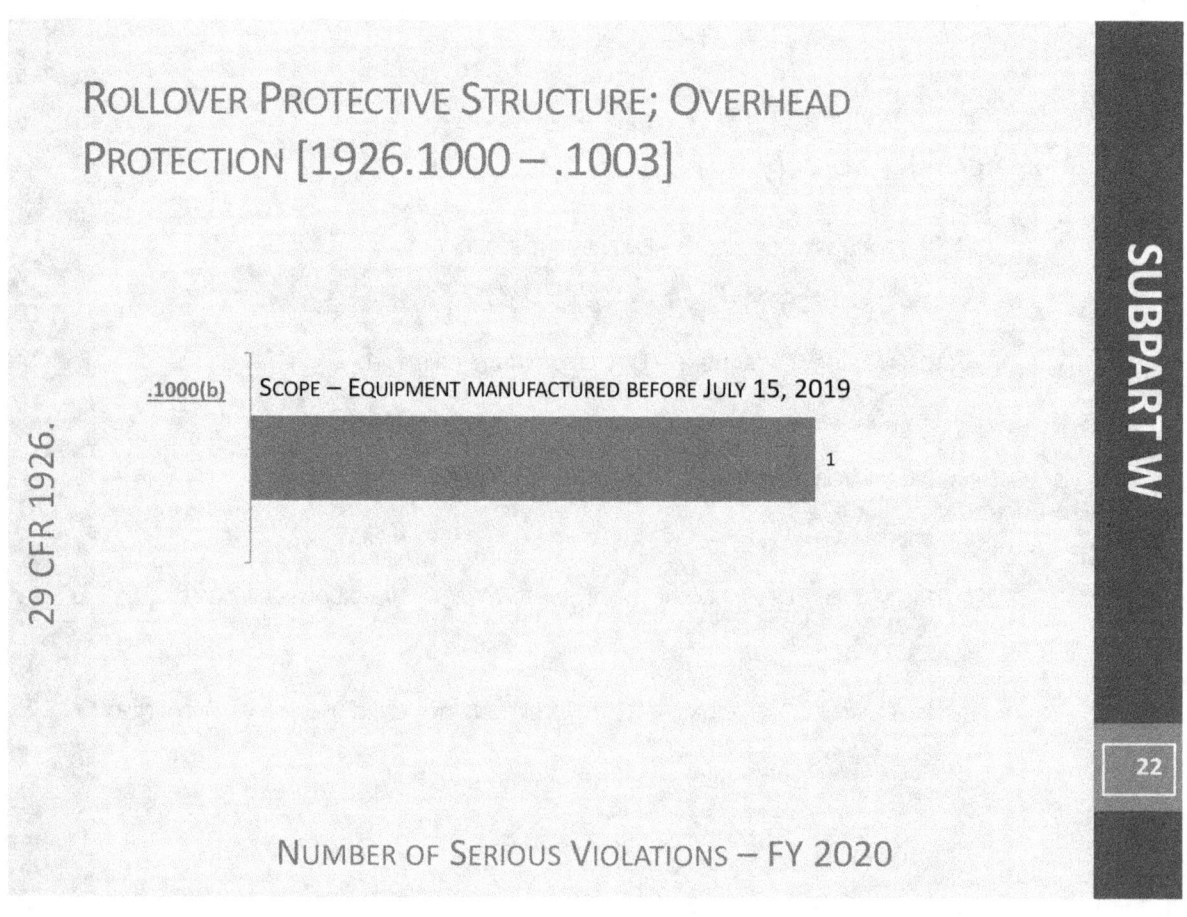

Stairways & Ladders
[1926.1050 – .1060]

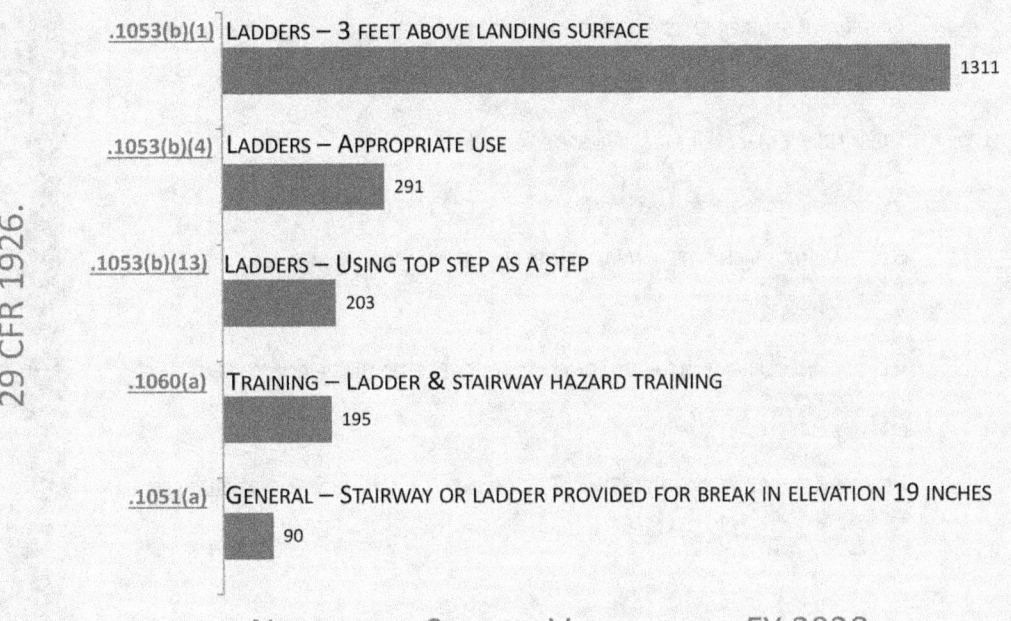

SUBPART X

Number of Serious Violations – FY 2020

- .1053(b)(1) Ladders – 3 feet above landing surface: 1311
- .1053(b)(4) Ladders – Appropriate use: 291
- .1053(b)(13) Ladders – Using top step as a step: 203
- .1060(a) Training – Ladder & stairway hazard training: 195
- .1051(a) General – Stairway or ladder provided for break in elevation 19 inches: 90

29 CFR 1926.

Toxic & Hazardous Substances
[1926.1100 – .1152]

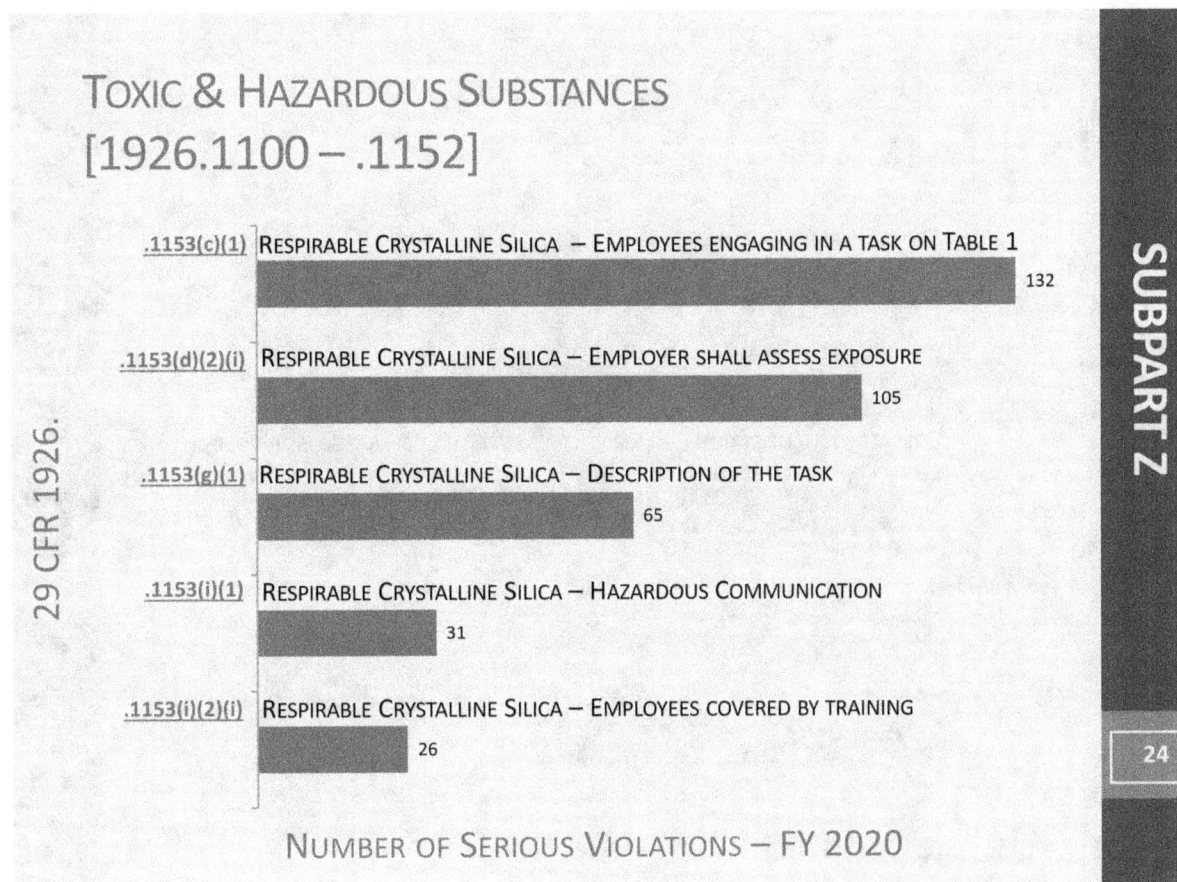

SUBPART Z

Number of Serious Violations – FY 2020

- .1153(c)(1) Respirable Crystalline Silica – Employees engaging in a task on Table 1: 132
- .1153(d)(2)(i) Respirable Crystalline Silica – Employer shall assess exposure: 105
- .1153(g)(1) Respirable Crystalline Silica – Description of the task: 65
- .1153(i)(1) Respirable Crystalline Silica – Hazardous Communication: 31
- .1153(i)(2)(i) Respirable Crystalline Silica – Employees covered by training: 26

29 CFR 1926.

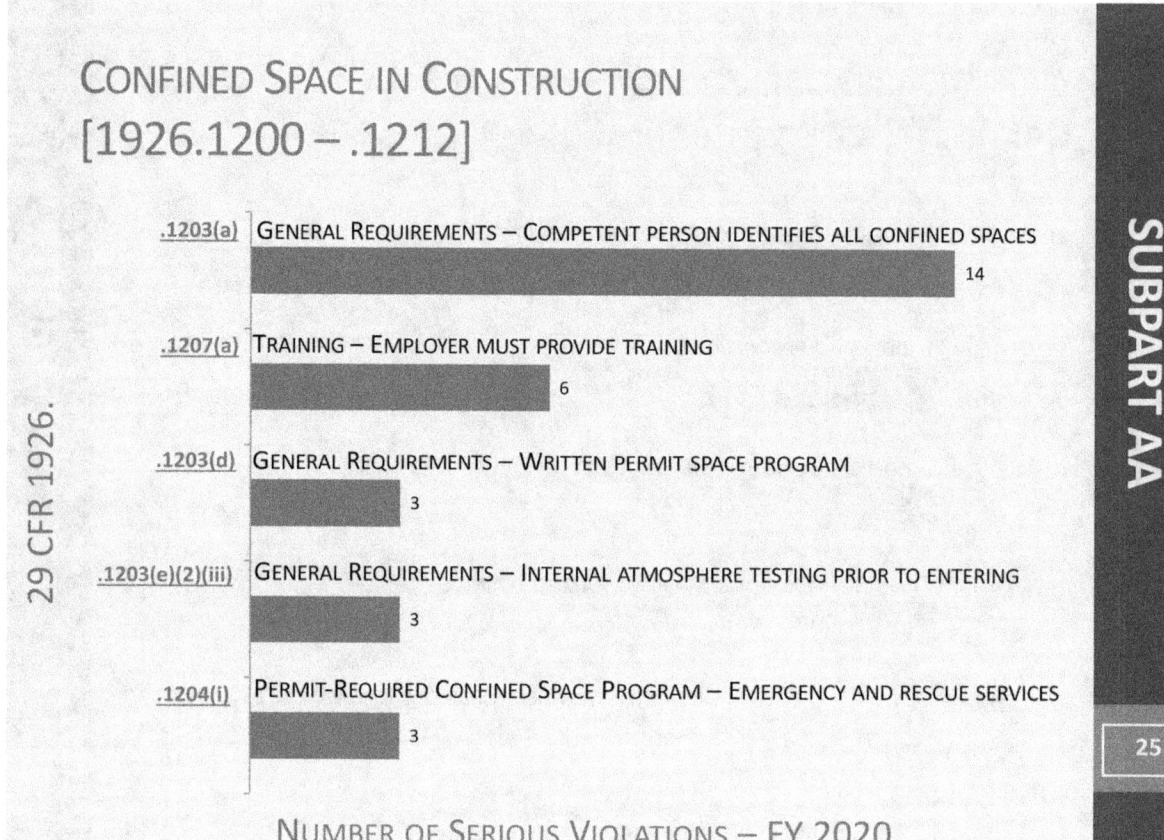

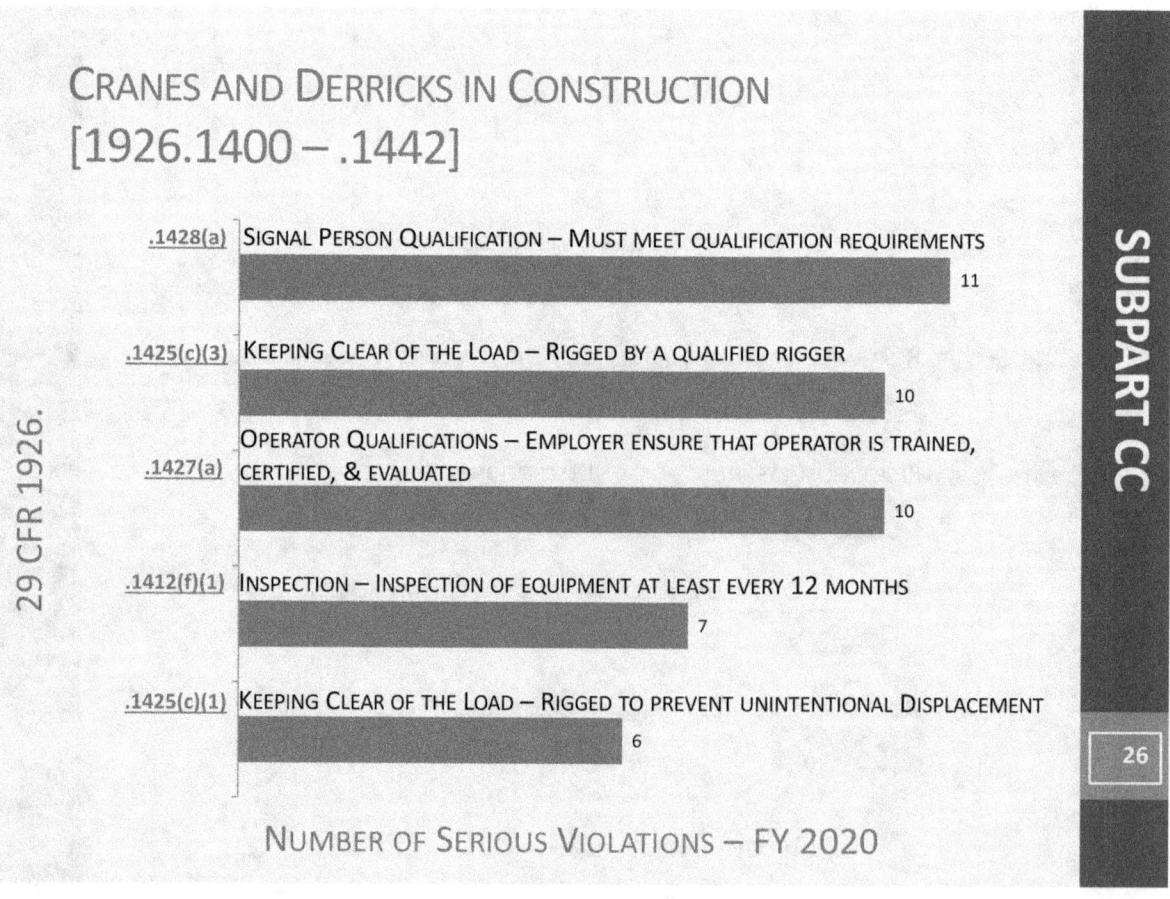

Other publications from the same author

General Industry

OSHA 10-Hour General Industry; Student Workbook
(ISBN 978-1979408592)

OSHA 10 horas industria general; cuaderno de trabajo para el estudiante
(ISBN 978-1719168144)

OSHA 30-Hour General Industry; Student Workbook
(ISBN 978-1719167451)

OSHA 30 horas industria general; cuaderno de trabajo para el estudiante
(ISBN 978-1719168328)

OSHA #501 Trainer Course in Occupational Safety and Health Standards for General Industry: Student Handouts
(ISBN 978-1721283255)

Construction

OSHA 10-Hour Construction: Student Workbook
(ISBN 978-1546484363)

OSHA 10 horas construcción; cuaderno de trabajo para el estudiante
(ISBN 978-1974103553)

OSHA 30-Hour Construction: Student Workbook
(ISBN 978-1975997830)

OSHA 30 horas construcción; cuaderno de trabajo para el estudiante
(ISBN 978-1977837479)

OSHA #500 Trainer Course in Occupational Safety and Health Standards for the Construction Industry: Student Handouts
(ISBN 978-1721282388)

Guía para el uso de andamios en la construcción
(ISBN 979-8697354322)

29 CFR, Part 1926 Safety and Health Regulations for Construction
(ISBN 979-8592329296)

Search by author, title or ISBN in your favorite online bookstore